Growing Closer

Marie Chapian

Growing Closer

Guideposts

CARMEL • NEW YORK 10512

All names of people whose stories are shared have been changed, as have their situations, in order that privacy may be carefully protected.

Library of Congress Cataloging in Publication Data

Chapian, Marie.
    Growing closer.

    1. Interpersonal relations—Religious aspects—
Christianity.   2. Christian life—1960–
I. Title.
BV4509.5.C44   1986   248.4   85–14174
This Guideposts edition is published by
special arrangement with Fleming H. Revell Company.

TO Christa and Liza

my babes in arms, my toddlers, my little girls in bonnets laughing in the sun, my Girl Scouts, my Missionettes, my perfect speller in braces, my brown-eyed honors girl in ruffles, my seekers, my students going off to learn from other teachers, my explorers, my teen rebels, my discoverers, my finders, my licensed drivers, one flaxen-haired girl on a Moped, the other behind the wheel of a silver missile, my musician and artist, my best gifts from God

and my friends

Contents

Contents

PART TWO
GROWING CLOSER BY UNDERSTAND-
ING YOURSELF

Contents

PART THREE
STRATEGIES FOR GROWING CLOSER

Contents

Foreword

Not many of us enjoy being lonely. Without feelings of closeness to others we tend to withdraw into ourselves, alienated from the world. This book will help you learn about *you*, your needs, and how to fulfill them in order to have and keep truly rewarding relationships.

Each of us is capable of intimacy and bonding with other persons. We each have a capacity for caring, intellectual exchange, respect, and companionship beyond a superficial, elementary level. Giving and sharing of our truest selves combine to make us people to be close to. We were born with the ability to have fulfilling and rewarding relationships.

So what goes wrong? I've talked to hundreds of people over the last few years who tell me they're unhappy because of frustrating and unfulfilling relationships. The common question is, "What's wrong with me?" usually followed by an unspoken complaint against outside forces. It isn't surprising that we become lonely. We deny our capacity for closeness.

I have found that for many people it's not easy to get "unlonely." There is a struggle that takes place—a struggle with trust, self-doubt, fear, and dread of being hurt. It's not healthy to deny our needs, and when we deny or refuse to face our need for closeness, we can act in the strangest ways.

Without self-understanding we can literally destroy ourselves. I see people in the counseling office who are intelligent, talented, decent people, but they are lonely and feel alienated from a personally caring world. Each week I talk to people who tell me they feel utterly unloved.

In private counseling sessions we begin the intense and liberating task of self-discovery, which includes looking at our reactions, motives, feelings, wants, defenses, mistakes, and misbeliefs. That's what you'll be doing as you read this book. In order to be close to somebody, you need to know yourself and your needs. You need to know what messages you continually give yourself that you may not be listening to or aware of. Denying or ignoring a problem only makes it worse.

I'm in the position to see hurting people experience change and growth on a regular basis as new self-respect is gained. Young and old people alike come to the knowledge that the *capacity* to be close to someone is as important and valuable as the need to be close to someone.

I hope you will see yourself with open eyes and meet yourself anew as you turn the pages of this book.

I receive letters from readers who share with me the hurts and the triumphs of their lives. This letter typifies so many. It's from a woman who wrote me after reading *Staying Happy in an Unhappy World:*

> Marie, I'll never be the same again. Your description of a "Victim" fits me to a T. I've wasted so much of my life being unhappy when I didn't have to. You've taught me new skills and taught me these skills in ways I can understand. Thank you for showing me who I am and that I'm a worthwhile person. I feel like my life has just begun.

Nothing could be more rewarding to me than words like these. As you read this book you will learn new skills and understanding, seeing yourself as a friend and someone to be close to. You'll learn why you avoid love, why you crave it; why you have or don't have the closeness you want in your life. You will learn, if you take what is here for you to take, some valuable Growing Closer skills. You deserve lasting, enriching relationships. Even if you tell me you're socially okay now, I assure you it can be even better. You can learn how to keep what you have and at the same time, grow even closer to those you care about.

Growing Closer is divided into three parts: Part One answers the question What Does It Mean to Grow Closer? and gives you understanding into the needs and behaviors of others, as well as your own. Part Two is Growing Closer by Understanding Yourself. Here you learn to become a whole person through certain awareness skills, all based on solid biblical principles. Part Three is where the Strategies for Growing Closer can become an everyday reality for you. You will learn Growing Closer skills to last the rest of your life.

Writing this book has profoundly affected my life and made me reexamine my own wants and needs in relationships. I had to take a good look at myself, and sometimes I didn't like what I saw. I have a lot of learning to do on my own journey to Growing Closer. It's not an easy journey, this one. It's probably harder than any other I've taken. But every step has been worth it. I've grown. I've shared. I've learned. Above all, I've grown closer to my own friends and loved ones.

One thing this book has given me is a new picture of friendship, intimacy, and oneness with God. I want to love and be loved. I know you do, too. To love is our highest calling, our greatest gift, sometimes hardest task, but always our sweetest reward. The One who loved us first shows us how.

MARIE CHAPIAN

Growing Closer

PART ONE

What
Does It Mean
to
Grow Closer?

ONE

A
Basis for
Closeness

W e've all heard that to have a friend you have to be a friend. But what does that mean? People are always trying to tell us how to attract people to ourselves; advice clutters our thinking on how to listen, how to look terrific, how to initiate and carry on conversations, how to meet people, and how to be interesting.

But closeness requires more. An attractive listener who also talks well and is interesting could very well be a Hitler or a Jack the Ripper. The question is, what makes us people others want to get—and stay—close to?

Counseling offices are filled with mismatched couples, rejected lovers, abandoned friends, and lonely heroes. What went wrong for these people? The divorced couple who once craved each other's company now snarl and snap at each other over the telephone about child-care payments.

"We were so much in love," a man of thirty-five told me. "We were the ideal couple. Everyone wanted a relationship like ours. We were the model of a perfect marriage. Then little by little we grew disinterested. She became preoccupied with her own world of kids, crafts, and the house, and I felt as if she were talking to one of her girlfriends when she talked to me. She'd tell me about what was on sale at the store and how some kid down the street had just cut his first tooth. I just didn't care. I wanted to talk about my work, tell about what I was doing. But she wasn't interested. When we went out together our conversation wasn't alive and exciting as it once had been. We didn't talk about books or ideas or any of the things we used to. We stopped praying together, except at meals for the kids' sake. I began to think of my wife as a smug, fat cat in her soft, safe world of babies and shopping, and I was the financier. I thought of the home as *their* house. My wife and *her* kids lived there. I paid for it all."

Possibly this marriage never really had a strong basis for closeness. Their "ideal" early years may have been superficially idyllic. A couple can look good together, have fun together, and share meaningful talks, but there's more to genuine closeness. This marriage didn't survive, although I can't help but think that if they had sought counseling and worked at change and growth together, they might have become friends and fallen in love. The wife was devastated by the breakup because she believed giving up her career to raise *his* children and keep *his* house was a sacrifice of love—yet he felt intolerably lonely and alienated.

Closeness means companionship. It means being genuinely interested and open with each other. The idea that husbands and wives can be friends is relatively new, and that may be why we too easily accept being lonely in our own homes. Most of us grew up in homes where friendship between parents wasn't seriously considered or discussed.

Closeness begins with *wanting* to be close. It is followed by *daring* to be close: taking the risk of rejection and hurt by being vulnerable and open. If I want to punish those around me, I only have to keep my heart and feelings to myself. We alienate ourselves from others by sending the message "I will not give you *me*."

If I remain alone, even with others around me, if I insulate myself against expressing feelings, if I refuse to know others and be known, it's because I choose to. In the Bible, David and Jonathan were friends because they chose to be. The hermit monks in the hills of Tibet remain isolated because they choose to be.

Most of us are more sociable at certain times than at others. Sometimes I may not want to be with a friend, even a close one. At other times I may not want to be alone. Examining our wants is the first step toward growing closer to anyone.

Ask yourself these What and Why questions:

1. What do I want in a friend?
2. Why?
3. What do I expect in a close relationship?
4. Why?

A healthy basis for closeness is never an intense and desperate need for approval or attention. When you ask yourself the question "What do I want in a friend?" also ask yourself *why* you want certain things in a friend. Why do you want intimacy?

If your needs for friendship are out of a dire need for approval and acceptance, I admire you for admitting it. The next question to ask yourself then is, "What if I don't receive the approval and acceptance I crave?"

The person with dire needs has little to give except the acts and affection designed to *earn* approval. This kind of behavior is often mistaken as "giving" or "selflessness." It isn't. It's *need,* plain and simple. Genuine giving is never based on earning approval. I give to you because your good and well-being are important to me. I do not give to you to earn your approval. In fact, I give you the right to disapprove.

You can see why admitting your motives for wanting closeness is important. I have met people who remain in their state of discontent, apart from meaningful relationships, because they refuse to admit their dire need for approval. It's frustrating to be unable to earn what you crave from another.

Know Your Expectations

What you expect in a relationship is another crucial consideration. It is related to need. Often we don't examine our expectations. We're not taught to confront expectations because usually they are considered unimportant. "A friend is a friend is a friend," seems to be the idea. It is a defeating idea because it prevents intimacy and growing closer.

Look at the case of Rachel, who recently gave birth to her second baby. She had always been a quiet person, on the shy side, and didn't make friends easily. At church she didn't participate in the women's activities for one reason or another. "I'm nursing the baby," "I have to pick Tommy up from nursery school," "My husband needs me to run errands for him," "I think I'm coming down with the flu," were excuses which provided building blocks for isolation.

When I saw Rachel, she was a sad, lonely person with many fears. She often confused fantasy with reality. She dreamed of a best friend, someone to share her every thought with. I asked her what she expected in a friend.

"I want someone like me, someone who will call me up every day and who will want to be with me and talk and do things together."

"That sounds fairly reasonable," I said. "Friends do that. You deserve such a friend."

But then she continued. "The friend I dream of having will be just *my* friend. I want it as if we're just inseparable—we tell each other *everything*. I want her to be closer than a sister. No matter what, she'll be my friend. She'll always be interested in what I have to say and always be there. She won't want anyone else to be her friend except me."

Rachel's need for acceptance and approval was beyond her control. She fantasized acceptance coming from someone outside herself. Married to a rather insensitive, impersonal, and overbearing man named Ron, Rachel received very little personal reinforcement from their relationship. She cowered in his presence, tending dutifully to his needs but keeping her distance. Rachel's life was like living at the bottom of an empty bucket. It was barren, unrelated, and apart from the outside world around her. She kept to herself, relating only to the children, who provided her with her sole comfort.

Ron's life, on the other hand, was also a lonely and isolated one. He was unaware that his wife was terrified of him, and had the misconception that she was just a quiet person. When she sat silently beside him watching television in the evenings or at their meals, he figured she just didn't have much to talk about. He told himself she wasn't very smart.

Ron was unhappy and questioned himself about his masculinity. If he wasn't working or doing a special project at home, he was anxious and worried. He, too, wanted friends, but felt Rachel would wither to nothing if he weren't there to make sure things were going right.

Rachel was receptive to counseling and readily accepted my pointing out her unrealistic expectations. How could anybody be what she wanted? Her fantasies didn't even include the possibility of closeness with her husband. In time Rachel concluded that a friend was a person to enjoy without being possessive or demanding of that person. She decided to make a real friend of her husband, and changed the way she behaved toward him. She tried talking with him, telling him stories, sharing her thoughts and ideas. It was not easy because Ron corrected her, challenged her, demanded she think as he thought. He was accustomed to belittling her and treating her like a child. This was punishing to Rachel but instead of retreating, she held on and did not give up. She was determined to get through to Ron, no matter how long it took or how terrifying the task seemed.

Rachel and Ron had to learn how to be friends to each other. Rachel had to face Ron's overbearing ways boldly and express her feelings to him. She had to express her need for love and her discomfort at being *controlled.*

Ron realized they couldn't go on in their isolated world, where he ruled on a lonely throne. He let go of the misbelief that he and he alone held the power to keep his home functioning. He began to see Rachel in a new light and appreciate her for what she was instead of what she wasn't. He made positive choices to see Rachel as capable and intelligent. This in itself caused a great breakthrough for this couple. Their behavior became more reinforcing to each other.

By the time Rachel stopped nursing her baby, she and Ron were talking on a more than superficial level. They decided to face the outside world together, so they became members of the Young Married group at a new church. They have made new friends and have continued to grow appreciably closer to each other. They are still hesitant and afraid of being too vulnerable. In time, as trust and closeness grow, they may even become good friends.

Needs Without Skills

Ron and Rachel have a long way to go in the Growing Closer journey because they both think that fear and respect are interchangeable emotions. You cannot genuinely respect another person if fear is involved. Fear of a person is not the same as respect. A close relationship cannot be built when fear is present because a basis for closeness is respect.

Rachel and Ron's story makes me think of the millions of people who are stuck in similar situations. Caught in a web of needs without skills to break through to fulfillment, they go on hurting themselves and others. Starving for attention and love, they hunt for satisfaction in all the wrong places.

The last place we think to look when we're lonely and unsatisfied is in ourselves. We excuse our isolation by reliving past hurts and disappointments; we blame the world around us for rejecting our plans for love and understanding; we accuse good people unjustly for not meeting our needs and fulfilling in us what only God can.

In this book you will discover what makes you the kind of friend you are. Why do you choose the people you choose? Why are others attracted to you? What do you have to give? Why do people react the way they do to you? What makes you a good friend, a good lover? By the time you finish this book you'll discover why your relationships sour, how they can flourish, and most of all, I pray you will learn how to be closer to the one person you are never without: yourself.

In the next chapters we'll look at reasons you're attracted to certain people and not others, as you discover skills to break the loneliness cycle in your life.

TWO

What Attracts People to Each Other?

The process of developing relationships is one of the most important and challenging goals we face. Since nobody can live in total isolation, relationships are a vital part of our human existence. The kinds of relationships we form are numerous. Some people are only casual acquaintances to us; others become companions, intimate friends, or spouses. Some relationships last tenaciously and others take the road of boredom or distress. At times we may prefer being alone to having any relationship at all. We react differently to isolation, depending upon our needs and wants and whether or not isolation is voluntary or involuntary.

The Need for Privacy

Admiral Richard Byrd survived an Antarctic winter completely alone and suffered no impairment to his physical and mental faculties. Other people have sailed around the world alone in small boats without experiencing any psychological harm, enduring long weeks and months isolated from all human contact. These experiences are different from that of the prisoner placed in solitary confinement. The prisoner has no choice in the situation.

To him, "solitary" is punishment because it is forced upon him.

The need for privacy is the process by which we shift back and forth, seeking interaction and then avoiding it. The need for privacy often results from "interaction overload," when we're just plain socially exhausted. In normal circumstances, some people may prefer to live by themselves, whereas others prefer the company of a roommate or a spouse. Research has shown that people who voluntarily choose to live by themselves are judged as less socially desirable and less active (but also more organized and more efficient) than people who choose a joint living situation.[1]

The need for privacy varies. Some people have greater needs than others for the presence of people around them or for social surrogates such as radio and television. Very few people voluntarily choose total isolation for long periods of time.

The Need to Be With Others

Each of us has a drive to be with others, and some people have stronger needs than others. Some of the reasons we choose to be with others include:

- the value that other people have in helping us attain our goals
- the personal rewards of companionship
- the value of another person to give us a standard for comparing ourselves with others
- self-evaluation
- anxious situations

You may wonder why I include anxious situations. When we are in such a situation, we usually have a greater desire to be with others, particularly those who are in the same predicament.

No matter what the situation, we have one thing in common: we want to be liked and accepted.

Seven Reasons We Are Attracted to Others

Why do we like each other? What makes us attractive to someone? Why are we attracted to one person and not another? The following seven points give us deeper insight into why we are happier with others than alone.[2] We are attracted to others who:

1. *Have similar beliefs, values, and personality characteristics.* We like people whose attitudes and values appear to agree with ours. Most people dislike those who disagree with them. If someone's personality is like ours, the attraction is even stronger. One research study done back in the sixties, during racial tension in the South, showed that among the white and black people studied, white people preferred associating with blacks who had attitudes like their own rather than whites who had opposing attitudes.[3] If a person is stigmatized or of lower status, a dissimilar friend may be preferred. Dissimilarity in attitudes is appealing then because too much similiarity to an undesirable person is threatening to our self-image.

2. *Satisfy your needs.* People choose relationships in which their basic needs can be mutually gratified. Sometimes the result of this choice is a negative pairing, as when a very dominant person is attracted to a very submissive and passive partner. Our needs vary and can be met, for example, by the woman who offers her physical attractiveness, as well as the man who offers financial security as his contribution to a relationship. A more positive model for us is found in the words of Rainer Maria Rilke: "Love consists in this, that two solitudes protect and touch and meet each other."

3. *Are physically attractive.* An attractive physical appearance remains a determinant of success in our society. We are taught that "what is beautiful is good." Studies have shown that the highly attractive person is more likely to be recommended for hiring on a job interview or to have his or her work evaluated favorably. Most people also think that an attractive person is less likely to be maladjusted or disturbed. Twenty-three hundred years ago Aris-

totle wrote that "beauty is a greater recommendation than any letter of introduction," and his words seem to remain true today.

To some people there is prestige in being seen with a more attractive person of the opposite sex (as well as the same sex), but research shows most people prefer others whose level of attraction is similar to their own. We may sigh over the media's current heartthrobs, but in actuality, we usually choose someone in our personal life who is close to our own level of attractiveness. In making such choices, we combine the person's attractiveness with our own probability of being accepted.

4. *Are competent.* We are more attracted to people who are intelligent than to those who are not. Although physical appearance is the first thing you notice about a person, ultimately intelligence may be more important. When it comes right down to it, men prefer women who are competent and able. Reversing the "beautiful is good" notion, we now see that "what is good is beautiful," if intelligence is thought of as "good." When we describe people by positive sets of characteristics, including intelligence, most people judge intelligence as quite attractive. It is also a fact that intelligent people who make mistakes are more often excused for them than those who are not as intelligent.

5. *Are pleasant and agreeable.* People like people who are nice and who do nice things. Most people are attracted to others who are pleasant and agreeable above those who are withdrawn or rude. Consideration is not only a nice attribute to have but it is also unintimidating and invites us to interact. We are least attracted to people who are intimidating and imply negative consequences for us, such as unappreciative or dishonest persons.

6. *Like us in return.* We are attracted to people who like us. Liking and disliking are usually reciprocal. We tend to dislike people who dislike us. Two people who share their dislike for a third person will tend to be attracted to each other. "My enemy's enemy is my friend," is the maxim they prove.

7. *We see often.* We tend to like people who live close to

us better than those who are at some distance. As the song from *Finian's Rainbow* says, "When I'm not near the girl I love, I love the girl I'm near."

At a more scientific level, you'll notice that residents of an apartment complex are more apt to like and interact with those who live on the same floor of the building than with people who live on other floors or in other buildings. Simple familiarity is the reason. We become more attracted to the people we see most often. We are more likely to see people who live close to us than those who live far away, and just that frequency of contact may increase our liking for these persons.

Seeing a person, talking, sharing thoughts, ideas, and experiences all increase our liking for that person. The anticipation of seeing someone will increase our liking for that one, even if we initially disliked him or her. This means that we may even come to like obnoxious people when we know we must live with them or near them.

Why We Like a Person

Essentially we like people who make us feel good. A basic explanation of interpersonal attraction begins with the concept of *reinforcement*. Reinforcement is like reward. We like people who reward (reinforce) us and dislike people who punish us. When somebody does something nice for us, it is a positive or reinforcing experience. When someone says something unjustly cruel to us, it's like being punished. A reinforcer is a bouquet of flowers; a punisher is a slap in the face. A reinforcer is in these words: "Thanks for being on time. You're so thoughtful." A punisher is, "Why should I say thanks? You're *supposed* to be on time."

Attraction involves two people. I'll never forget something my brother told me after he met the girl he eventually married. He came home one night with a definite glow on his face. We sat together talking in the kitchen before saying good night and I asked him, "Billy, what attracts you most to Charlotte?" He didn't hesitate in his answer. "Marie," he told me, as though he had made a great discovery, "We *talk.*"

Talking and sharing are reinforcing and absolutely necessary for real intimacy. We look for people who will talk to us and listen to us. If you're not talking to the one you love, you are not experiencing intimacy as you deserve to. Talking does not mean griping and dumping out a ton of troubles on a person. Nothing destroys love quite as efficiently as complaining and moaning about life and its trials. If it's love you desire, it's important to know how to give your best. Your best is reinforcing, not punishing and negative.

But what is your "best" kind of love? We'll look at that in the next chapter.

THREE

Kinds
of
Love

Everybody talks about love. Philosophers and songwriters, novelists and poets have for centuries debated the meaning of love. How do you define it? It's easier to define *attraction,* which is basically evaluating a person or symbol of that person in a positive or negative way,[1] but definitions of *love* are more complex.

There are two kinds of love that we are going to get to know and understand: *passionate* (romantic) *love* and *companionate love.*[2]

Passionate love can be defined as "a state of intense absorption in another." Sometimes lovers are those who long for their partners to provide their complete fulfillment. Sometimes loved ones are those who are ecstatic at finally attaining their partners' love, and momentarily experience what they perceive as complete fulfillment. Passionate love includes intense physiological arousal.

In contrast to the intense feeling of passionate love, there is a second form of love: *companionate love.* This is the affection we feel for someone with whom our lives are deeply intertwined. In contrast to the sometimes momentary state of romantic love, companionate love reflects longer-term relationships and may or may not be a romantic relationship.[3] Your best friend, your wife, uncle, or cousin could be a companionate love in your life. Let's look at these two kinds of love, starting with passionate love.

The Measurement of Passionate Love

It is difficult to define *love* but it is easier than trying to scientifically measure it. Several years ago, social psychologist Zick Rubin created a love scale to measure degrees of romantic involvement.[4] He included a liking scale in his love scale and presented it to 158 couples at the University of Michigan who were dating but not engaged.

The love scores of men and women for their respective dating partners were almost identical. However, the scores showed that women *liked* their dating partners significantly more than men liked them in return. This difference is due to the fact that women rated their partners higher on task-oriented points such as intelligence and leadership potential.

Men and women reported liking their same-sex friends equally, but women indicated greater love toward their same-sex friends than did males. The results of this study show that we make a definite distinction between liking and romantic love, but *liking* did not prove as strong a motivating factor in permanent relationships and marriage. Can you believe it? *Liking* each other is what keeps love alive in any relationship. We spend time learning how to like and communicate with a best friend, but the spouse doesn't get the same investment of energy. In this respect, romantic or passionate love by itself falls short.

The first stimulant to romantic love is *physiological arousal*. We describe these feelings as "butterflies in the stomach," or dizziness, light-headedness, a tingling sensation, all of which give us the idea we are feeling romantic. When you feel breathless and slightly off balance, you may interpret this as a sign of love. One man told me that when he met the love of his life, he was so overwhelmed he felt like crying. Once I overheard a young man tell his mother, "Every time I'm around Marilyn I feel as if I'm going to get sick." His mother hushed him by saying, "Oh, Norman, you're just in love."

A second stimulant to romantic love is *similarity*. Attraction, often confused with love, needs time to prove itself. If you're going to fall in love and stay in love with your current loved one, develop similarity. Similarity of two partners is an aid to a long relationship. People with similarities in age, education, intelligence, attractiveness, and goals have more in common than people who are not similar in these areas. If you're not similar in these areas, develop your own similarities. I've seen a mutual love and zeal for God transcend cultural and age differences. I've seen couples torn apart by lack of similarities, lack of communication, and a great fixed chasm of differences separating them make great changes. The force that changed them was the presence of a living God in their lives.

One example of this is the relationship between a couple I'll call Susan and Jim. Jim was twelve years younger than Susan. She grew up in Yonkers, New York; he was born and raised in Puerto Rico. She was a women's lib aficionada and he was a male chauvinist. They were married because Susan became pregnant and they thought it was the best thing to do. After the wedding, they created a nightmare. Their apartment was filled with broken items they had thrown at each other. They fought constantly. Then they decided to let God into their lives. They opened their hearts to Jesus Christ and began learning about love and a life of goodness and genuine caring. They began to think with God's mind, feel with His heart, and see each other with new eyes. Little by little they fell in love and began to respect and cherish one another.

Their little girl became their blessing instead of their curse. They developed similarities in interests, activities, thoughts, ideas, prayers, goals for their lives—God showed them, through His Word, how to have hearts of love instead of selfishness. Now their feelings for each other are experienced, without pretense or sentimentality.

Sentimentality is a form of romantic or passionate love. It is not a positive manifestation because it doesn't build up anyone or anything in a healthy, constructive way. Its essence lies in the fact that love is experienced only in fantasy and not in the here-and-now relationship to the other person, who is real. The most widespread form of sentimentality is in the vicarious love satisfaction experienced by reading magazine love stories, listening to love songs, watching TV soap operas, and patronizing love stories in the movies. The unfulfilled desires for love and closeness cause you to find satisfaction in unrealistic ways. As long as love is a daydream, it exists in full bloom, but as soon as it comes down to the reality of the relationship between two real people, it becomes frightening and unappealing. Everyday duties such as balancing the checkbook, doing laundry, and changing diapers can be interpreted as intrusions and obstacles to true love.

Love's Nourishment

Love needs to be nourished. Passionate love, which includes physical arousal and sentimentality, often has no skills—just *feelings*. Companionate love, on the other hand, is the opposite. Over time, a couple's expression of love for each other can stop if companionship, affection, moral support, and interest decrease. Earlier intense romantic feelings shift and change, creating a less fiery companionate relationship, and one or the other of the partners is bound to feel disillusioned.

Allan Fromme writes:

> The lover sees more in his loved one than anyone else sees. He adorns her image; he exaggerates her beauty of body or face or personality. He puts into it what may not even be there but no matter; he wishes it there, he sees it there, and he loves her for it.[5]

This is passionate love. It is wonderful, but it can fade. Fromme goes on to say that quite often the romantic lover creates a completely nonexistent image of the loved one. He hardly knows the real girl. He is in love with his ideal image of her, or of someone he would like her to be. The loved one does the same with the lover: she loves what she thinks he is, or wishes he is. This relationship can only deteriorate and fall to pieces with their broken illusions. What they need is a good dose of companionate love.

Most people see the idea of love primarily as that of being loved, rather than that of loving, or of their capacity to love. Love then becomes a problem of finding ways to be loved, to be lovable. One way, which is used especially by men, is to be successful, to be as powerful and rich as one's position permits. Another, used especially by women, is to concentrate on physical attractiveness.

People work hard to be loved. To some it is an all-consuming occupation. Many of the ways people try to become lovable are the same as those used to become successful or to win friends and influence people. One of the first Growing Closer rules is this: *Love is not earned.* You don't win love like a lottery or a game. You don't earn it like a promotion or good grade in school. If you can't see yourself as lovable now, you won't see yourself any more lovable once you've *earned* someone's affection. You'll only worry how to keep yourself loved and you'll become fiercely jealous and competitive with those of your same sex. It will be as though you're always at work earning, earning. And you'll never know when you won't be good enough at earning and someone will take your prize away.

Nobody Loves Me

Feelings of alienation and isolation are enemies of a love relationship. The feeling that "nobody loves me" and "nobody understands me" usually indicates that the person who feels unloved is one who is not loving and not giving love. A person who feels misunderstood generally does not understand and does not try to understand others. When passion fades, a person may interpret it as being unloved. Absence of sentimentality may seem like rejection. It is here the skills of companionate love must be put into practice, or a relationship can become an unflattering mirror.

Another enemy to a lasting relationship is excessive ambition in one of the partners and not the other. A person who feels possessed by a drive to succeed is already in love. The man who wants to make millions of dollars is in love with that idea, that goal. If a woman is in love with fame and recognition, she will have little room to love a friend with the intensity that person may want. Ambition is admirable, but if it is excessive it may show that the individual is not loving of other people. Often young people who are starting out in life will have opposite ambitions, and it becomes vital to learn companionate love.

I believe two people experience companionate love because they are already companions to themselves. Accepting yourself at the center of your existence means to invest the necessary learning it takes to get to that place.

This book is dedicated to learning the skills of becoming closer to yourself as well as to others. Erich Fromm said the proof for the presence of love and the depth of a relationship is in the aliveness and strength in *each* person concerned, and this is the fruit by which love is recognized. Though Fromm may not have realized it, this is the fruit God gives us, too: individuality, aliveness, and strength because He lives in us. All of our loving one another develops from our relationship or nonrelationship with God. He teaches us what companionate love is because that is how He loves us.

Companionate Love

It is God's nature to love, as it is His nature to give Himself constantly in love. Love is the personality and essence of His being. He *is* love. Everything we know about love and beauty, God already *is;* and He gives Himself to us.

The Apostle Paul wrote that we are to be *rooted* in Christ (Colossians 2:7), which means the same as to be rooted in *love*. When we give ourselves to God, receiving Jesus Christ as Lord and Savior and lover of our lives, we then are in a position to look at relationships as He views them.

A strong example of companionate love is that of David and Jonathan: " . . . the soul of Jonathan was knit with the soul of David, and Jonathan loved him as his own soul" (1 Samuel 18:1). David was a much-loved man. His soldiers died for him. The Bible speaks of Hushai as David's friend and also of Hiram, king of Tyre: " . . . Hiram was ever a lover of David" (1 Kings 5:1). David said he was a companion of all who fear God and keep His precepts (Psalms 119:63).

Companionate love, in order to be its fullest and most sublime, must be grounded in a mutual love for God. Two people with a strong love for God will be able to understand the principles of love. God *is* love. His Spirit runs through our veins, our blood, our personalities.

Look at the relationship between Elisha and Elijah in the Bible. Elisha had been a farmer all his life. When Elijah came to him, Elisha was plowing in his father's field behind twelve pair of oxen. Elijah threw his cloak over Elisha's shoulders, indicating he was to follow him. Elisha asked only that he be allowed to kiss his parents first. He then made a stew of a pair of oxen for the people, and left on his new calling.[6] Elisha became dedicated to Elijah like a son to a father. He served him, ministered to his needs, and refused to leave his side. He sacrificed all to serve God by becoming Elijah's student and successor. Theirs was companionate love of the highest order because their foundation was solidly fixed on the Lord.

Jesus' example of companionate love is unparalleled in all of history. The Son of God becoming a human being for our sakes is the highest love known to us. In His life He loved people with such a rich and compassionate love that one would have to be totally insensitive to miss it in the New Testament. Even the ridiculing Jews sighed, "Behold how he loved him!" when Jesus responded to the news of the death of His friend Lazarus (John 11:36). He "loved his own," the Apostle John wrote (John 13:1).

Priscilla and Aquila made quite a team for the Kingdom of God. There isn't a character profile in the brief mention of them in the Bible, but in the sentence Paul writes about them, we learn much about their relationship and their common love for God and serving Him. Paul wrote of them that they "have for my life laid down their own necks: unto whom not only I give thanks, but also all the churches of the Gentiles" (Romans 16:4).

The word *eros*, the Greek word for "passion" or "romantic sexual love," is not found in the New Testament at all. Eros is not a horrible evil and should not be neglected in a love relationship. Eros does have a rightful place in the Christian life. Passionate love between a man and a wife is certainly wonderful, holy, and enriching. The Song of Solomon couldn't be more explicit in extolling the wonders and joys of passionate sexual love.

But whereas eros seeks to fulfill its own hunger, companionate love speaks more of *agape* love, which is the Greek word expressing a love that seeks to give. That's companionate love.

Companionate love is also camaraderie, or *philia* love, which is based on intimate friendship. In medieval times nature, emotions, and the body were considered base and nontrustworthy. They were thought to endanger our souls. Passion and inflamed desire were thought to be emotions for lesser beings, not for those who treasured beauty and development of the spirit and soul. Friendship, then, had a high and noble value placed on it. In today's culture, passion is more extolled than friendship; nevertheless, friendship is necessary if we are going to survive as lovers.

Lovers can be friends, but friends do not have to be lovers. Companionate love includes passion. It is emotional. It is the expression of feelings in words but is not restricted to words alone.

Understanding one another is a trademark of companionate love. Whereas romantic or passionate love may use communication to compete or hotly disagree, companionate love never competes. It allows for disagreement, enjoys it. It is playful, trusting, compassionate—not threatened with differences.

Jesus tells us He wants to call us friends. We're His friends, He says, if we do as He asks. Abraham was called a friend of God (James 2:23), and Jesus tells us how we can be, too, when He says:

> "No longer do I call you slaves; for the slave does not know what his master is doing; but I have called you friends, for all things that I have heard from My Father I have made known to you."
>
> John 15:15 NAS

These words give us a glimpse of the sharing, giving heart of God. "We're friends because you take what I give you," He seems to be saying. "I can tell you things and share with you what is most important to Me. Everything My Father has taught Me I give to you. You are My friend."

Samuel Johnson said, "That kind of life is most happy which affords us most opportunities of gaining our own esteem." I can't think of anything more healthy to our esteem than to be called a friend of God.

When you think of friendship, what do you think of first? When you see it through the eyes of companionate love, every relationship can be brought into a new depth of awareness and closeness. Let's look closer.

FOUR
Best Friends

While most of us are busy pursuing romance and married love, our need for real friendship is often neglected. In some societies friendships are the most important relationship to be had. They are valued above marriage and all other relationships.

In certain societies, the decision to be friends is often formalized by elaborate rituals and ceremonies which are major events of the culture. Robert Brain writes about the Bangwa of the Cameroon, where he spent two years studying and researching.[1] To the Bangwa, having a friend is as important as having a wife or a brother. "Best friends" continually verbalize their affection and give each other gifts, accompany each other on journeys, and demonstrate their affection in many overt and covert ways. If boys or girls are not given best friends by their parents, they choose their own. They create songs of praise about their friends. During annual ceremonies at the palace, male friends dress in full warrior gear and greet one another on the dancing floor, striking each other's swords in the air as a public demonstration of their friendship. Interesting, isn't it, how we choose to remain aloof and apart, yet inwardly we all long for a friend? Can you see yourself asking a friend to come clank swords with you?

In Polynesia and Melanesia friendship is a close and strong bond also. The Trobriand adolescents who are best friends embrace in public, sleep together, walk around the village arm in arm, and the friendship goes on into adult life.

When I was in Nigeria, Africa, in 1980 I was charmed by the displays of friendship and affection of the people there. Small boys walked down the road holding hands, men embraced and touched each other in the course of a conversation. Men who were best friends would rub each others' stomachs as a sign of friendship and affection. When I became friends with some of the women it was as if we were one, sharers of something lasting and precious. I'll never forget being asked to go to a prayer meeting by a new friend: she spoke sweetly into my ear while kissing my face.

It was new to me, this unabashed and pure expression of friendship, and I was stunned by the innocence and loveliness of it.

I realized how isolated we Americans can be, smiling at one another politely in church and then returning home alone to our TV sets, video games, stereos, cassette players, radios, and personal computers. In my altogether too-short stay in Africa, I felt the clear message of "We're here together—you're important and so am I—we share the same God—you're me and I'm you, and yet I'm me and you're you."

It was much later, while doing my research for this book and studying friendships of other cultures, that I began to see our society as the exception in a world where friendship is a social and psychological need. Blood pacts are common in certain societies. To celebrate friendship and bond them for life, two friends will mix their blood in a most reverent ceremony. Others attend as witnesses and they are then expected to share meat when one has killed an animal, eat meals together, help protect each other's families, pay each other's debts, bury each other as well as each other's relatives, and never be offended by one another. Can you imagine making a vow to never be offended by a person—and then keeping it?

Can Men and Women Be Best Friends?

A primary requisite for best friends is absolute equality. This is another reason men and women best friends aren't as common in our society as same-sex friends. In order to be true friends, there must be equality. Absolute respect is necessary.

In relationships between men and women, one or the other often takes a dominant "protector" role. Among the men and women I interviewed, I discovered a woman considered a man her best friend at times when she was going through some peril—whether psychological, emotional, or practical. "Bill came over with his truck, moved all my things out of the apartment, and loaned me money to rent another place. He was the best friend I had at the time. We're still good friends. I know I can always count on him."

Or consider this statement: "Jim and I are the closest of friends. He is always there, like a big brother, watching over me to make sure I'm okay. I have to get his approval on the guys I date."

Here's another: "Shirley is a really great friend. We've known each other since we were kids. She's always there when I need her. She always has a listening ear and a shoulder to cry on when things go wrong."

And: "Wanda is really a good, good friend. In college she did my laundry for me and typed my term papers. If she doesn't approve of some girl I'm dating, chances are I won't go out with the girl anymore. Wanda is one person I really trust. She's more of a sister than a sister."

Notice the distinct "protector" clues in each of these testimonies. Other statements I heard were, "He [or she] is the one I call when I'm in trouble." One young woman's best friend performed all the manly functions she felt unable to do. He repaired her car, fixed the lock on her door, carried heavy packages, and helped her buy a stereo. "He's the best friend a girl could have," she told me.

In a healthy relationship, some protecting or parenting

of each other is interchangeable, depending on needs. A relationship founded on need and that remains in the needy-protector mode is not a real friendship as I define it. Equal footing is missing.

To have an equality-based relationship doesn't necessarily mean we must be the same size or age or have the same abilities, but it is necessary to have a strong bond of equality in some primary area of life.

What Is a Best Friend?

Research shows that women tend to be closer to women friends than men are with one another. Women tend to need women friends more and relate on an intimate basis more freely than men do. Whereas men will think they're close buddies because they hunt together every year, women consider a close friendship as being able to talk about personal things.

Men and women usually have a similar number of close friends, although women have closer and more frequent contact with their friends and relatives than men do. Opposite-sex interactions are always more publicized, but affiliation with someone of the same sex is very important to our personal growth, particularly for women.

Men's closeness with one another is usually centered around an activity or a shared interest to talk about. These relationships are important to a man and reinforce his sense of self and sexual identity. When a man and woman are platonic friends, it usually is based on a shared interest, as well.

Cal and Jana are close buddies and have been for about five years. They are both artists. They work together daily in the same art studio. Jana told me, "I fight and compete with my boyfriends and my brothers, but with Cal it's different. We don't fight. And he genuinely wants me to be a success in my work. We respect each other enormously."

What cements Cal and Jana's friendship is a common interest and genuine respect for each other. Two important factors in any friendship are: *need fulfillment,* the degree to which the relationship fulfills each individual's personal needs, and *likeness* of values. The more we agree on important matters, the more we tend to befriend each other.

The persons we are most comfortable with and whom we like best are usually people a lot like us. They enjoy doing what we enjoy; religious and political views are similar, or at least tolerated with respect. Our hopes, dreams, fears, and ideals are similar and appreciated. These are the people we understand and are most comfortable with. We feel confident when we are with these people because we feel that we are understood in return.

Research has shown that likeness is so important to friendships that people often overestimate the degree to which we are alike. It's the values that count most. If our values are similar we will be closer friends. Cal and Jana are close friends because of their values. They both have a passion for art, share each other's ideals and goals, and intellectually communicate on a level stimulating to them both. They meet important personal needs for one another.

"There will never be a romance between Cal and me," Jana told me. "We have decided to be friends and friends only."

Cal and Jana consider themselves best friends. When a man and a woman become "just friends" it means they have found that special level of communicating that feeds them both as friends. It would insult them to give their relationship a sexual connotation. It is an unfounded and irrational idea that physical contact has to be sexual or that men and women can't be friends.

When a Friendship Goes Bad

We are not bound by law to keep a friend when we don't want to. We can end friendships whenever we feel like it. Though friendship is a basic need, we move, change jobs, leave town, divorce one another, and our needs go on seeking to be fulfilled. Close, loving contacts between individuals are basic needs. In order to discover our completed selves we must have friends—not distant, superficial acquaintances, but *friends.*

A twenty-eight-year-old man told me about a friendship he had with a woman his age. "We can talk about everything under the sun. She is very talented and stimulating," he told me, but as of late he was becoming more and more irritated with her. They had been good friends for two years, but certain developments had begun to take their toll on the relationship.

"With all her wonderful qualities, she complains constantly," he told me. "Sometimes I feel as if I'm with my spoiled kid sister again. I want to shake her up and tell her to stop being so self-centered. But I don't want to hurt her feelings. That's why I don't tell her how I really feel, or how she wears on my nerves with her problems."

This woman's behavior fits the description of what I call "dumping." It is when one partner unloads all of his or her emotional garbage onto the other in a vain attempt to find answers or relief.

I knew this relationship could only head downhill unless some changes were made. If they had been planning marriage, it would have been disastrous. You need to be wary of playing psychologist-parent roles in a relationship. If you are stuck in these roles you'll find yourself on a pathetic merry-go-round, trying to come up with suitable answers for your poor, hurting child-patient. If you finally wear out and explain you've had it up to here, your child-patient will feel abandoned and neglected. After all, you've taught him or her that it is okay to dump problems, worries, complaints, and other emotional garbage on you. You've never protested before—why now, all of a sudden? Your requests for relief or outside help will be taken as a sign that you are a selfish and uncaring person.

"Dumping" is not the same as sharing. When people become friends, it means they have met at a level of communicating that feeds them both. They are equal in giving and taking. If you approach friendship with a bag of hang-ups so big you can't get it through the door, you'll dump those problems out on the person closest to you. That person, even if he or she is flattered into believing he is capable of handling the dumped-upon role, will eventually disappoint you. Nobody can meet such huge demands or come up with the solutions you crave.

The more whole and complete *you* are, the better friend you make. When you are whole and complete in yourself, you don't make emotional demands on someone else, don't insult a friend with bitter complaining, and don't destroy the beauty of life with unrealistic cravings for happiness.

Some relationships are founded on common complaints, but these relationships are not very happy or enriching. You don't feel happy when you're with a person who complains, and when you become ensnared and join in with your own list of woes, you make yourself doubly unhappy.

Friendships That Last

On the other end of the spectrum are Claude and Mavis, both in their seventies. They have been friends for fifty years; they knew each other in college. They were friends with one another's respective spouses, shared the joy and pain of child rearing at the same time, as well as illnesses, family traumas and victories, weddings of each other's children, and they cried with one another at their spouses' funerals. Now, still neighbors, they remain the closest of friends. They go out, play cards, attend church, garden, and talk. There is a common respect and love between them that does not include romantic attraction.

"Well, sure I love Claude," Mavis told me. "He's the best friend I've ever had—more like a brother than my own brother."

Such a simple answer regarding a lifetime relationship. I had heard people who knew each other only two days express their feelings in more glowing terms. Her reference "more like a brother" interested me. I told her I had a brother but I didn't want anyone else to ever take his place or be more like him than he was to me.

Then she opened up. "Well, Marie, it's like this. Claude *is* a brother to me. He's a sister, a cousin, an aunt, and an uncle, too. He's every friend I've ever wanted and every child I've ever loved. He's my teacher, my student, my pal. We don't allow each other the luxury of old-people talk. We don't fuss or worry. We've had enough trouble in our lives. We understand each other. We appreciate each other. He has his house and I have mine. We're not lonely enough or stupid enough to get married."

Marriage often offers an antidote for loneliness and emotional uncertainty. But we ought not discard the value of rewarding friendships which provide us with great satisfaction. Some people latch onto an eligible person, thinking sharing life with the same house and hearth will be the answer to all problems, when being *friends* could be far more fulfilling.

Elaine, a sixty-five-year-old widow, said, "I put up with Ralph's snoring for thirty-seven years; I don't think I want to start all over with someone else." Elaine had met and become friends with a widower her age. He proposed to her and Elaine was not eager to accept. "Compared with knowing someone for thirty-seven years, this guy is a relative stranger. And he'd be snoring in *my* bed. Then there's the question of agreeing about what to watch on TV, where to go on vacation, how to spend our money, whether or not the dog sleeps in the living room or on the porch, whose kids are the rudest, and how high we'll keep the heat turned up."

Married people may feel they have to stay together even though they despise one another. Friends are different. In order for them to remain friends they must share common liking and respect for each other. When a friendship turns sour, the friends usually part. Married people can live in the same house without sharing the simplest courtesies or kindnesses. Friends won't put up with such behavior. They simply move on to other friendships that are more rewarding. True friendship won't tolerate alienation or abuse. Many married people have no concept of friendship with their spouses. "I love him, isn't that enough?" one married woman asked. The answer is clear: "No, it's not enough. Become his friend."

I have asked scores of people the question "What does a friend mean to you?" Below are some of the answers I've received. After you read the list, check off the descriptions that fit a relationship you already have in your life.

1. A friend is someone I can call at hours of the day I wouldn't call anyone else.
2. A friend is someone who sees me at my worst but never forgets my best.
3. A friend is a person I can always find interesting.
4. A friend is someone who thinks I'm a little bit more wonderful than I really am.
5. A friend is someone who I can be quiet with and who I can also talk nonstop with.
6. A friend is someone who doesn't forget about me when away doing something more fascinating than what we've shared together.
7. A friend is a person who is as happy for my successes as I am.
8. A friend never makes me feel guilty if I don't call.
9. A friend doesn't compete with me.
10. A friend doesn't scratch my dog's stomach if he knows I haven't in a long time.
11. A friend doesn't give me advice and then make me feel bad when I don't take it.
12. A friend trusts me enough to say what he really means when talking to me.
13. A friend doesn't try to know more, act smarter, or be my constant teacher. A friend is a *friend*.
14. A friend is someone who diverts my attention from the cares of life, who reminds me that life can be fun and happy.
15. A friend is someone who doesn't try to change me.

A friend is on my side and takes time to know and understand me.

16. A friend is a person who listens to me even when he isn't particularly interested in what I'm saying. He listens because he sees it's important to me.

If you can check off more than three of the answers as descriptive of a current friendship in your life, you're a blessed person. Now go back over the list and check off the descriptions of a friend you'd *like* to have in your life. This second list of checks will be much longer than the first. It's rare to meet a person who has even one "ideal" relationship. In our world of progress and growth, we have missed out on the value of growing closer to each other. You can change that for yourself now.

One man told me, "I've worked at getting an education, pursuing goals, meeting deadlines; I've labored hard at trying to achieve a level of excellence in what I do, but I see very little, if any, investment in growing closer to a person. I have grown closer to goals than to people."

A woman in her thirties told me, "I don't keep friends very long. I guess I must come on too strong. I'm always looking for someone to talk to, so that's how I spend my time. I'm either calling people, trying to find a friend, or I'm talking the ears off someone. I don't think I've accomplished much in my life, but I've done a lot of talking and crying on people's shoulders. I hate to be by myself and I can't shake the feeling that no matter who I'm with, I'm alone."

In these two examples you can see the absence of the Growing Closer kind of understanding. Neither the man nor the woman knows how to grow closer and stay closer to a person. When I've looked at the broken dreams and shattered relationships of people like them, I've asked why. Is there something we can unlearn, relearn, or learn afresh to make us closer? I think the answer is yes.

PART TWO

Growing Closer
by
Understanding
Yourself

FIVE

Starving
for
Attention

Loneliness can be a positive emotion if it brings you to a better awareness of yourself and your needs, and leads you to positive action. It's good to be lonely if you are aware of the messages you're giving yourself by the very feeling itself. If you're lonely in a crowd, lonely with the people you are supposed to be closest to, lonely when alone, lonely in your work—these can all be positive pieces of information. You can then stand back and take a good look at yourself, your choices, and the patterns you've adopted that are now malfunctioning. Most of the time you don't want to do anything about your loneliness except find a person, persons, or activity to fill the gap and make the pain go away.

When a person craves attention and admiration, something precious of the self is lost. Nobody was born to accept his or her identity as an extension of somebody else or to forfeit their own personhood to pay for acceptance.

What Is Fulfillment?

A single woman in her twenties told me in exasperation, "I hated being lonely so I went back to school at night, joined a singles club, and started going out more. But I'm *still* lonely. All these activities make me busier, but I'm not fulfilled."

This woman was lonely in spite of a busy and active life. Busyness is a poor substitute for a meaningful, loving relationship. God will provide awareness of His vast world of possibilities if you will choose to have a close relationship with Him.

In my own life, the thought of singleness after being married was almost more than I could stand. The idea terrified me. My whole identity was wrapped up in the word *married.* I was forced to come up with a new identity as a single person and I hated it. I stalked the rooms of our apartment as though I were pacing heaven's corridors. I cried out to God. It took time, but little by little I learned that it was a relationship with Him that would give my life the richness and delight I ached for. No amount of busyness would give me what I was born to have: a loving friendship with God. That was seven years ago, and the friendship gets better and richer every day.

You don't have to be single to find this out. Loneliness is a feeling you can have no matter who you are or how busy your life is. I meet and talk with famous men and women who are loved and adored by millions but go home to face loneliness.

When We Can't Be Satisfied

"Good friends are hard to come by," sighed a vocalist whose records have sold in the millions. "Friends say they love you, but who knows?" A famous and much-envied person, she felt alone and unwanted. I wondered if the problem was that she didn't believe her friends loved her *enough.*

If you're a person who *craves* love and are starving for attention, you will paradoxically be unable to receive the love offered you. The person in a starve mode doesn't believe anybody loves him or her quite enough. The affection of friends isn't perceived as deep enough. Loyalty of loved ones doesn't seem true enough. Love is just never enough—there is always something wrong or missing. Nothing is satisfying. Your demands are unrealistic and will keep you detached and cut off from intimacy.

The person starving for attention is usually a dependent person with an unfulfilled need for someone to completely depend upon.

People in the limelight are often motivated more by a passionate desire to please others than they are to feel genuinely good about themselves. When you are motivated to please others and receive approval, you become a slave to the whims of others. You'll never be pleasing enough to feel good about yourself.

How do you recognize these motives to get approval? The answer is to be brutally honest with yourself. Ask yourself, if your efforts for approval were rejected by others, would you feel defeated?

When you crave attention because without it you feel empty, you are in a starving pattern of existence. Friendship is difficult in this mode because you pay such a high price for it. You *earn* it instead of allowing yourself to be respected for who you are. With such efforts on your part to win friendship, it is nearly impossible for anybody to give back to you what you desperately crave. It is simply too much and too demanding.

Friendship is not an expensive piece of jewelry that you go into debt to buy. It is not something you pay a huge personal price to attain, such as selling out your personal worth. Friendship and closeness are natural products of being an open and compassionate person. If you're a Christian you've got the Spirit of God within you, and it is God's nature to be giving and loving, yet uncompromising. Christian people are likable because the personality of Jesus is within us through the indwelling of the Holy Spirit. To crave the love of a person and trade off self-awareness as well as God awareness in the deal is to quench your ability to love and be loved as you deserve.

Working for Approval in Your Business

A man named Ed told me, "It's just not true that I'm trying to win approval from others by my hard work. I'm not in a starving mode. I *love* to work hard. I do it for myself, not for others." Then something happened to show him otherwise. A co-worker received a larger bonus at Christmas than he did, and he was crushed to the bone. "I can't understand it. I've worked so hard. I've put in overtime for no extra pay; I've taken work home at night; I've always done more than was asked of me. This is a fine way to show appreciation. I'm so mad I feel like looking for another job."

What Ed didn't realize was that while he enjoyed working hard, he also wanted *approval*. When he told me he loved hard work he was telling the truth. But he didn't love it for the work's sake or for his own sake—he loved it because he hoped it would earn him approval. He thought he would get rewarded for all his efforts. When the reward wasn't there, he felt he was being punished. It is true that we must earn the approval of our superiors if we are to receive promotions and make advances in our careers. It would be naive to assume we could be successful without approval. I am talking about *longing for* approval; living for it.

When you *crave* something, you're out of balance with reality. When you crave attention, approval, or love, if it is not forthcoming, you feel betrayed and punished.

"After all I did for her, now she just goes off and leaves me without a leg to stand on."

"I can't believe he could do this to me. I've done everything I could to help him get ahead, and now that he's finally reached his goal, he dumps me."

"I've worked hard in that class. How could the professor give me only a *C*?"

All of these statements indicate living in the starving mode.

Jack shocked his friends and parents by quitting college in his junior year. "I just don't think it's doing me any good," he said casually, as though it shouldn't affect anybody else's life. "Besides, I can always go back later. Think of the money my parents will save. I just need a little vacation from school."

It wasn't really a vacation from school Jack needed, as he discovered through counseling. He was worn out from trying to win the approval of others. He was usually more overworked and stressed than his roommates at college, not because he studied harder but because he worried more. His state of anxiety was so great it often immobilized him. He spent many days out of each semester sick with various maladies ranging from sore throats to intense lower-back pain. His girlfriend often wrote his papers and finished his class assignments while he slept or sat stilted beside her, worrying about whether or not she'd finish on time. Fear of failure and anxiety about doing poorly were his enemies.

In talking with Jack, I learned that since he was a boy in grade school he never considered himself bright or capable of doing well. He had an above-average IQ, yet a dread of schoolwork overwhelmed him. His parents didn't have an inkling that all during high school Jack had other people doing his work for him. He got by and gained approval, but he hadn't gained self-esteem.

Now let's look at these two men: Jack, the student, and Ed, the man who didn't get the bonus he expected. Would you choose to have a close friendship with either of these men? Ed worked harder than was required of him in order to gain approval, and Jack avoided work because of the possibility of failure. Both valued approval too highly. Jack was willing to sell out his integrity by allowing others to do his work, in order to get by and avoid losing approval. Both of these men needed other people to affirm their self-worth. When the reality of their personal emptiness struck, their response was the same: they wanted to run, quit, get away.

The Starving Person and the Provider

Are you drawn to people with needs for approval? Do you feel your heart tug with yearning to help when you hear words like these: "Nobody cares about me"; "I'm just a failure"; "I'll never be anything"; "I can't finish what I set out to accomplish"; "I don't know what's wrong with me"; "I try and try but nothing ever works out for me."

If you can answer yes, you fit into the pattern of someone I call the "Provider." Providers are people who earn approval by helping the helpless. Often the Provider's help does more to encourage dependence than build character in the person being helped. Since the Provider needs to help others in order to feel a sense of worth, he keeps up the pattern, never allowing the dependent person a chance to grow and experience independence.

People with strong dependent needs are always looking for a Provider, someone to rescue them from this cruel world, someone else to give their lives meaning or value. The dependent person doesn't want to face the thought that he or she may not be or have what others expect, so continual reinforcement is necessary.

The dependent person is never truly convinced of his or her worth. No success seems great enough unless someone else is cheering him on. Relationships aren't fulfilling if the other person doesn't play the Provider with constant supportive acts and words. The dependent person always needs someone else to say, "Good job" or "Well done" or "You're special."

The dependent person is what I call a Starver. He or she really is starving because there is no end to the hunger for approval and support provided by others.

The Provider feeds the dependency needs of the person stuck in a starving mode. "Oh, but you *are* smart." "Why, it's just not true that you can't do anything right." "You're so wonderful, so clever. You should be so proud of yourself."

The Provider takes on a parenting role, a superior role. The needs of the Provider are not to feel important and necessary but to feel *superior*. "You are feeling bad and I'm not. That makes me superior and you inferior. You need me and what I have to offer you, therefore I'm superior," is the message.

If you are a Provider, when your inferior person no longer needs you, you'll find another to take his or her place. That's Beth's story. She became involved in a relationship through the mail with a man who was serving a prison sentence. When he was released they began dating. His needs were overwhelming and she was right there to help in every way she could. She loaned him money and gave him her car to use. She listened to his complaints and fears by the hour and convinced herself she was doing her Christian duty. She helped him get an apartment and a job. She cooked for him, took him to church, and before long they were engaged. Two months before the wedding was to take place, he told her he wasn't ready for marriage and was moving back to his hometown to start a new life.

Beth bristled with anger for a while, feeling betrayed and used. But before long she was involved with a man she met at work. He was an alcoholic. It became Beth's cause to help him overcome his problem. She helped him get into a treatment center, went to AA meetings with him, took him to church, cooked for him, cleaned his apartment, and even got him into a physical fitness program. One day he told her he had met another woman with whom he had fallen in love, and he hoped Beth would understand if she and he remained "just friends."

"It was like getting shot in the back," Beth said. "What a pushover I must be."

Providers and Starvers are alike because they don't trust their own worth. "I'm nobody without you," is the song they both sing. Beth's next experience was with a young woman she met at church who didn't have a place to live and was out of a job. Beth took her in and befriended her, loaned her money, gave her the use of her clothes and car, and set to work at helping her straighten out her life. The young woman basked in the attention Beth gave her, and to outsiders it appeared that Beth's selfless labors were paying off. The young woman succeeded at landing a job; she became more involved in church activities and seemed happier.

But Beth wasn't happy. "My life is not my own," she complained. However, when the young woman moved out on her own, Beth took it as a rejection. "Why does everybody leave me?" she asked. "Why don't I have friendships that *last*?"

Beth didn't know it, but she had answered her own question. Her life was not her own because she chose to focus all her attention on the needs of other people in order to: (a) not face her own and (b) earn approval. Beth did not know how to choose lasting, solid relationships with *equal* give-and-take. Beth's relationships, which were based on need, could never give her the fulfillment that a relationship based on equal respect could give. Being close to a person does not mean one or the other must be helplessly dependent.

Nobody benefits by weakness. Feeling powerless creates a need to please in order to feel secure. Trying one's wings, daring to fail, and taking risks are too threatening to a person whose security is shaky. The irony is that such dependency upon others for approval breeds hostility and resentment toward those depended upon. It is not uncommon to resent the one you most desperately want to be close to. These feelings can be compounded by guilt because, after all, the person is so good to you. Beth's friends felt guilty because they couldn't give her what she wanted, which was for them to remain dependent so she could continue to play the role of Provider.

The Provider's ego may be enlarged by the superior role he or she plays in a relationship with a dependent person, but the benefits sour eventually. Nobody wants to remain dependent, and Providers can become bitter and disillusioned, too.

Men often fear dependence to the point of acting aloof and detached in a relationship. Many women who are emotionally involved with men have a common complaint: "I don't know if he really *likes* me." It's not that he doesn't care—it's that he has the misconception that closeness or intimacy may render him dependent. This is threatening to his masculine identity. He doesn't realize this, of course, unless he faces himself openly and dares to name his fears.

Dependency is destructive when we seek to find ourselves in somebody else. You are dependent as a Starver because you crave the constant approval and support of another person. You are also dependent as the Provider, because you must have the dependency of the Starver in order to feel worthwhile. Both of these roles are filled with frustration and dissatisfaction. Many suicides result from Starver/Provider behaviors. The situation can become so bad that, as one woman put it, "I saw no answers in sight. I didn't think there was any hope for me at all. I just knew nobody would ever love me as I needed to be loved."

A Provider whom I counseled said, "When my wife no longer needed me I wanted to end it all. I felt completely drained of the energy to go on living. What was the use? I was a nothing." Fortunately, these two people found help before it was too late.

When Dependency Is Positive

Our dependency is only in its proper place when we realize our need of God and His wisdom. We can afford to be dependent upon God because He gives us the fulfillment we crave. Another person cannot fill God's shoes. He gives a special knowledge of our value that no person can. It's a truthful evaluation—no flattery, no lies. God shows us by His love for us that nothing can defeat us, wipe us out, or deceive us unless we allow it to.

If you think you fit the dependency mode either as the Starver or the Provider, you can take charge of your life now and start anew. Say out loud, "Jesus is my Lord and Savior. I do not have to strive for approval and love from others in order to feel worthwhile."

To become utterly dependent upon the Lord is to become free from the clutches of self-doubt and aching for constant attention. Jesus told us, "Abide in Me, and I in you. As the branch cannot bear fruit of itself, unless it abides in the vine, so neither can you, unless you abide in Me" (John 15:4 NAS).

These are words of love and acceptance. He continues, "Just as the Father has loved Me, I have also loved you; abide in My love" (John 15:9 NAS). We are accepted by God. Tell that to yourself. Tell yourself to listen to the voice of the Holy Spirit, who tells you the truth instead of the lies you are inclined to believe. His word to you is always one of strength and encouragement. Despairing and fearful words are not in His vocabulary. They don't have to be in yours, either.

Release yourself now from the old, cruel, self-destructive habits. Pray with me, "Father, in the name of Jesus, I choose to be free. I choose to be the real me, dependent only upon You. I renounce any neurotic dependent pattern and choose to receive strength and encouragement from You."

Now read Romans 8:15.

The Power of Commitment

In the story of Ruth in the Bible, you see a woman who had been utterly dependent upon her husband and her husband's family for all her needs. The women in Ruth's time had few resources available to them to provide a living other than through a husband. A woman either lived in her father's house or got married. There were no female doctors, real estate agents, corporate presidents, or lawyers in Ruth's time.

Ruth's husband died. Her mother-in-law, Naomi, was also left a widow. Ruth followed Naomi back to Israel, away from her own people in Moab. She could depend only on God now. It was a great triumph of faith when Ruth told her mother-in-law, "Whither thou goest, I will go; and where thou lodgest, I will lodge: thy people shall be my people, and thy God my God" (Ruth 1:16). Without her fully being aware of the power and impact of her commitment, Ruth became a partner with God to fulfill His desires and plans for all mankind.

Ruth trusted the Lord of her mother-in-law and became the great-grandmother of King David and a predecessor of Jesus Christ. If she had remained grief-stricken, stayed in Moab, worrying and trying to find her solutions in people, we would never have heard of her.

No person can fulfill your need of God. Beware of looking for a person to take the role of God in your life. The Lord won't fail you, but people will because no human being is flawless.

You can trust God. He understands your wants. He understands your needs. You can afford to be totally dependent upon Him. There is no need of yours that escapes His eye; there is no desire, no fear of yours that He is not concerned with. He is watchful of His own. He is saying to you now, "Come. I'll be your friend forever."

SIX

Getting
Beyond the
Externals

Sylvia is a thirty-four-year-old woman who has been married to Jeff for ten years. She is suffering from feelings of guilt and confusion and tells me, "I don't understand it. I have been married to Jeff all these years and I still don't know if I love him. He's a successful man and a good provider. He's honest, clean, and not moody. You just respect a man like that. I respect Jeff, but why don't I feel that I love him?"

Sylvia could have been talking about a stranger. "The problem is, I don't even know him," she said, as if reading my mind. "I feel so guilty to say this, but I just don't think I love him. It's so hard to admit. I can say I *respect* him, though."

Sylvia only thought she respected Jeff. I can say I respect the President of the United States, but I may not know that person at all. *Respect* means more than "admire." What Sylvia was really saying was that she approved of her husband's behavior; she found his attributes socially approvable—but acceptance and approval of a person doesn't mean love. It may be one of the stepping-stones toward love, but in itself it does not constitute love. There is a big difference between approval and respect. Respect is more than approval. Respect is being able to say, "I trust you with all that matters to me because you

62

are worthy." Respect is vitally important to an intimate relationship.

If Sylvia really respected her husband instead of merely assigning him her approval, she would have had feelings closer to love. To receive esteem and honor means someone has looked beyond the external, further than the obvious and into the depths of you. I'm always amazed at couples who don't bother to look closely at each other. Their lives are controlled by superficial appearances.

Sylvia was a person who did not look beyond the external appearances and behaviors of her husband. But Jeff made that easy. He confined his conversations to the concerns of the day such as bills, what was for dinner, did she want to see a movie? He kept all conversations informative or centered around activities. They talked about what could be seen, touched, tasted, smelled, and heard, but did not relate on a level of commitment where their whole selves were on the line to be valued, understood, reassured, comforted, protected, and believed in.

Jeff and Sylvia were gracious and likable people who did the right things and said the right things, but always had a nagging feeling that they were missing out on something. Sylvia confided, "Jeff seems like a person you're *supposed* to love. He is the kind of man Mom always wanted me to marry. If Mom were alive, she would approve of Jeff."

Talking with Jeff was another story. He was doubtful of counseling and told me right at the start he didn't think it was necessary. Later he contradicted himself.

"Jeff, what's your definition of *respect*?" I asked.

The question took him by surprise. "Well," he began, "I guess I respect the person who accomplishes things." He went on to tell me he could respect persons like Helen Keller, Jonas Salk, Henry Ford, and Colonel Sanders. I asked, "Do you think your wife is a person who accomplishes things?"

"Sylvia?"

"Yes. Do you respect her for her accomplishments?"

"I don't see that she has anything to do with it."

"Do you like to be respected?"

"Well, sure, who doesn't?"

"What about your wife?"

"You keep bringing her up. Sylvia's a wonderful person and a good wife, but she doesn't *do* anything. I think we would both be happier if she got a job or went to school— you know, if she *did* something with her life."

I asked him if he had ever shared these feelings with Sylvia.

"I wouldn't dare," he answered. "She doesn't like it if I break the mold. Every time I have tried to express feelings that are different from hers, she has gotten upset. I've always got to be the nice guy who never upsets her apple cart. I put on a smile for all occasions and everything's fine. As long as I keep being the nice guy I can live in peace."

The Release Click

Something took place in Jeff at that moment. It's what I call the Release Click. It's like a key clicking in a lock— suddenly a door is flung open and a whole storehouse of feelings is released.

My question about respect only served as a tool for the Release Click. What Jeff and Sylvia were saying was that they didn't know each other. There are two rules I always give people at my seminars as well as in the counseling office. The first one is this:

Never guess what is inside another person. When you guess, you could be wrong. You may think that when a person is quiet he is angry. On the other hand, you may think when that person is quiet, he has nothing to say. Both guesses could be wrong. Don't guess. Say something. The second rule is this:

Put words to your feelings. Always *say* what you're feeling and ask what it is you want to know. It's okay to ask, "Are you angry?" "Do you want to be quiet now, or is this a good time to tell you a funny story I heard today?" Don't guess what someone else is thinking or feeling, and be careful not to come up with your own reasons a person acts a certain way. You don't want to put yourself in the position of being a mind reader, and you probably don't want someone else to think he can read your mind, either. These two rules apply to friends as well as spouses.

Sylvia and Jeff needed to get to know each other. In order to do that, there had to be an open and responsive atmosphere, created by both of them, in which they could be free to open up and be themselves. They were not accustomed to sharing their feelings, their hopes, and their dreams. They never discussed the future, and rarely talked about the past and present. The change was difficult for them both, but eventually they began to relate on a level of closeness they had never known before.

Sylvia confessed to Jeff her fear of being hurt. They needed to learn that as the bond of togetherness became stronger between them, so would their capacity to be hurt and to hurt each other. This would mean they were close to love.

Getting beyond the external requires being vulnerable. It means trusting yourself and your own feelings. Here are three Growing Closer points that Jeff and Sylvia had to face:

1. Look at the two sides of yourself—the side you show others and the side you show only to yourself.
2. Do you believe that only certain kinds of people and certain behaviors are lovable?
3. Do you see yourself as lovable regardless of the bad points?

Being afraid to express your feelings and to let your thoughts and hopes be known can only lead to the slow and painful demise of a relationship.

Another example of an external relationship is quite different from that of Jeff and Sylvia. A man I'll call Arnold is a brilliant forty-one-year-old businessman who has been involved in local politics since receiving his graduate degree from a large eastern university. For years his dream was to hold public office, and recently he had an opportunity to make his dream come true when he ran for mayor of his city. Arnold was the most qualified of the candidates for the job. Those who knew him and his political record supported him with a passion. There was just one problem: Arnold was not a warm, receptive person. His manner was curt and businesslike. Even at home, he treated his family with cool detachment. He loved his wife and children but spent very little energy or time getting close to them. They knew him much in the same way his employees and co-workers knew him: externally.

Arnold's campaign was a clean, vigorous one and he worked tirelessly around the clock until election day. There was great enthusiasm among his supporters, and judging from the preelection surveys, Arnold looked like a winner. But he didn't win. His opponent won by a landslide, and Arnold was devastated. The man who became mayor was far less qualified, but he was an outgoing, mudslinging personality who made unrealistic promises which the public bought. Arnold didn't take the loss well. Even his family was surprised at his response.

He became morose and bitter, spending long hours alone, not wanting to be with his friends or family. Losing to a person whom he felt wasn't qualified for the job was like a personal failure to Arnold, a blow against his very personhood. His attitudes became hostile as he harbored feelings of being misunderstood and unappreciated. He lost his self-respect and doubted his ability to succeed in anything.

Arnold was a Christian man with high ideals, but now he wondered if even God had turned His back on him.

Nowhere to Go for Emotional Support

At times of loss, our emotional needs are very strong. Arnold needed encouragement and support as well as the compassionate concern of a significant person or persons.

It is important to know where to go for the support. Arnold felt as if he had nowhere to go, which means he went to the wrong places. The kind of person you need at times of intense emotional struggle is a supportive one with whom you share equal respect. Two mistakes to avoid making when you experience loss and you need help are these:

1. Don't confuse a supportive person with the Provider we spoke of earlier, the latter being a person with a need to feel superior. You'll only feel worse about yourself when you talk to a Provider because the Provider will appear to have all the answers and to have learned all of life's lessons, whereas you will be the one with no answers, floundering around in the elementary school of life. A supportive person can be an understanding family member or a close friend. Your next choices would be a caring therapist or a concerned pastor who can spend time with you.

2. Don't turn to impersonal, noncaring persons for advice or commiseration. The bartender at a local pub or the waitress at the lunch counter are not persons to share your deepest feelings with. I've seen people pour out their souls to total strangers they meet on a bus or at a party. This behavior is not showing how open and honest you are—it's just plain dumb.

Arnold's losing the election turned out to be a blessing in disguise. If he had won, he would have gone on indefinitely in the same external, impersonal manner. The price for his professional step up would have been his personal happiness. Arnold was willing to pay that price, but now he had second thoughts.

I spent many hours with Arnold, talking about his life and his goals. His political dreams were largely based on a neurotic need for power. One day he told me, "You know, Marie, I'd never have come to you if I had won that election. It kind of scares me to think I've been a nonperson all my life. I haven't had an identity outside of my political ambitions."

The Click That Counts

Arnold's wife, Joan, was an energetic, feisty woman the same age as Arnold. Joan had no resentment for Arnold's love affair with his career. She had learned in the early days of her marriage to develop her own personhood separate from but including her husband. While Arnold was in graduate school, Joan helped support the family by working as a teacher's aide. She later went on to earn her degree in education and became an elementary school teacher. Teaching, taking care of a home and three children, and an active social schedule filled Joan's life.

At our first meetings, Joan wanted me to get the impression that she and Arnold had an ideal marriage. "Arnold is a good man," she carefully explained. "We have always gotten along well. We hardly ever argue. He's come up the hard way, working his way through school and all, but I've been right there with him. When I went to school he helped out at home with the kids. It's been a real good relationship."

Joan was hurting but didn't want anyone to know about it, possibly even herself. One day I asked her about their sex life. Then the Release Click I spoke of earlier happened. A storehouse of feelings tumbled out.

"We don't have sex. I don't know why. I think it's because I don't appeal to him anymore. Maybe he has found someone else, but it doesn't make sense. He's always home moping around. Who would want him? I'm confused. We never did have the greatest sex life, but at least it was something. Do you think I should lose weight? Maybe I should start a fitness program and get back in shape. I just don't know why we don't communicate. I feel so old and frumpy. Arnold doesn't treat me like a woman. I'm just a thing around the house—a *thing*."

They lived in a world of externals, he busy achieving and she trying to keep up with him. Meanwhile, the years were going by. She was beginning to feel old and unwanted. He suffered a loss that plummeted him into self-doubt and a true identity crisis. They would never be the same again.

Breaking the Shell

Many times it is a crisis that pulls us out of an external pattern of living. A divorce, death in the family, or a severe loss of some kind can force us to take a long, hard look at ourselves and make us evaluate where we've been and where we're going.

I have discovered that persons with a close relationship to God have an easier time breaking their external shell and becoming more vulnerable to love and commitment. All of us were created to love and be loved, but the person who has given his or her life to God in Jesus Christ has spiritual health as well. How much of that help you want is up to you. There are those who are Christian only in name and others who are pressed so closely into the heart and mind of God, they actually think and behave like Him, bearing His personality of love, kindness, and forgiveness. With Jesus Christ as the center of your relationships, the external shells break. I will long remember the afternoon Arnold and Joan sat in my office holding hands and praying together like little children on the eve of a fabulous voyage. They dedicated themselves to each other and to God. With tears in his eyes, Arnold said, "We've gone to church for years, but this is the first time we've ever really prayed together."

I heard from Arnold again recently. He is in business for himself and enjoying it immensely. He told me he feels as though God has given him a whole new lease on life. "The hunger for power is just not there as it used to be," he said. "I feel I've missed out enough on life. The Lord is showing me what it's like to really be alive." With his commitment to God, he was able to commit himself to his wife, family, and friends. He came closer to himself and his own needs and found he could accept himself on any level of achievement.

The Solid Foundation

God accepts us on all levels of achievement. Hunger for power, a drive for control, needs for approval and for keeping our emotions on an external level will always rob us of true happiness and the ability to have rewarding relationships.

Jesus said, "All who listen to my instructions and follow them are wise, like a man who builds his house on solid rock. Though the rain comes in torrents, and the floods rise and the storm winds beat against his house, it won't collapse, for it is built on rock" (Matthew 7:24, 25 TLB).

With a relationship to God solidly formed, like building a house on a rock, your life can take on a dimension of spiritual ability you never dreamed possible. God becomes your *friend*. You don't have to prove anything to Him. He loves you unconditionally and is concerned about you as well as your relationships. God has sliced His arm and tied it to yours. His blood pours across your skin and into your veins. His Son, Jesus, has laid down His life for yours in order that you can be a son or daughter to Him.

When the reality of God is yours, and you are bound to Him, your life will be forever altered. Because of your friendship with God you can be free to appreciate yourself as He sees you, free to value yourself as important because He does. You can now have compassion and mercy on yourself and open yourself up to loving and giving to others.

Being a Whole Person

Whole people are for the most part at peace with themselves and the world. Whole people make the finest friends. A whole person, as I see it, is one who has been made whole by the love of God. It is through His love for us that we get a true picture of ourselves as He sees us. We then become able to love and receive love because we receive from God a strong sense of our own value and importance. A whole person is one who won't demand that others fill in the missing pieces in his or her life, knowing that only God can do that. Isolated people living in an external world don't have a crucial sense of importance or value. Without this sense, we aren't really whole.

Here are four reasons we settle for living externally:

1. *We have been hurt in the past.* This is the false notion that your past mistakes are going to be repeated. Because you were hurt before, you never know when somebody might hurt you again. You protect yourself by living on an external level which includes laughter, fun, and lots of activities to protect yourself against anything deeper. You look at the people in your present life as the people of the past. You're reminded of the negative experiences of the past by comparing people who are now in your life with those who used to be a part of your life. "He's just like my dad" or "This place reminds me of the awful place I used to live," are statements linking your present world to the negative past. In order to combat this misbelief, it is important that you take the Word of God as your source of truth. "Therefore if any man is in Christ, he is a new creature; the old things passed away; behold, new things have come" (2 Corinthians 5:17 NAS) is your reality.

2. *We see ourselves as failures.* Your own self-respect is vital to your very existence. Without it you can do the most destructive things and not even realize what you are inflicting upon yourself. You will seek friendships which only punish you. You might even choose a marriage partner who reinforces your feelings of failure. Instead of seeing yourself as having the ability to learn from your past mistakes, you see yourself repeating them. You define the behaviors of other people according to your feelings of failure; for example, you want to have instant acceptance from someone and when it is not there, you feel responsi-

ble. It is important to separate yourself from the past. You can admit your failures, not with a sense of hopeless despair but with the realization that failure was the result of treating yourself in a self-defeating manner. It is time now to learn how to live a victorious life. " . . . *new* things have come," is the truth now.

3. *We don't think we're as good as others.* I have talked to far too many people who have not resolved feelings of shame. "Others are better than me," is the unspoken feeling. It is a powerful failure motivator. "I'm not as good in work, or not as good in love, or not as good in life," is the misbelief. Feeling that you are not as good as others causes guilt, which always asks to be punished. You can hurt yourself physically and emotionally because you think you deserve it. You will choose relationships that are guaranteed to hurt. The Bible tells you, "When He, the Spirit of truth, comes, He will guide you into all the truth" (John 16:13 NAS). The truth is that God is rich in His mercy because of the enormous love He has for you (Ephesians 2:4).

4. *We see ourselves as better than others.* This false notion is yours when you are afraid to see yourself as you really are. It is as if looking at yourself realistically would cause you to discover you are a real nothing. Not true. The false notion is that if I'm not BIG I must be very tiny. See yourself in the light of your true potential. As a child of God you were created to give and receive love, joy, peace, patience, kindness, goodness, gentleness, meekness, and self-control. Your imagined fears can be combated when you identify them and begin to work at eliminating them from your life. No one is better than you or worse than you. Respecting yourself is not the same as puffing yourself up to unrealistic expectations. This will only bring you feelings of defeat and bitterness against a cold and unappreciative world. You will always feel obliged to reject others before they reject you, which will make you a lonely and isolated person.

Releasing ourselves from the confines of an external way of life is not as difficult as you may think. Even the most dyed-in-the-wool externalized person can change. The bond of intimacy grows between people who reach out to each other and attain fulfillment by communicating and sharing on a level of appreciation that goes beyond what we see or hear. This takes creative energy—the kind God gives you. Now you can watch your masks drop, one by one, and your relationships grow into beautiful and free expressions of warmth and genuine love. The next chapter will help you decide which masks you wear.

SEVEN

Masks
as Obstacles to
Growing Closer

An attractive twenty-eight-year-old secretary named Monica sits slouched in a chair in my office. She stares at the wall and angrily asks, "Marie, if I'm so lovable, why do I feel so ungratified?" Then she adds with a hopeless note in her voice, "If only someone would come along and make me feel better about myself."

Monica's complaint represents countless other ones I hear regularly. I call them the IF ONLYS. You might be reciting some of your own IF ONLYS. They sound like this:

- IF ONLY people would accept me as I am.
- IF ONLY I could find friends who didn't have problems.
- IF ONLY I had more time to meet people.
- IF ONLY I weren't shy.
- IF ONLY I were more handsome [prettier], I'd be more lovable.
- IF ONLY I had finished college, I wouldn't feel so inferior.
- IF ONLY other people were as open and honest as I am, then I could trust them.
- IF ONLY I could find someone to depend on.
- IF ONLY I hadn't ruined that last relationship. It

was probably the best thing that ever happened to me.
- IF ONLY people weren't so critical.
- IF ONLY the world weren't so corrupt.
- IF ONLY I had more money.
- IF ONLY I could lose weight.
- IF ONLY I had different parents.
- IF ONLY people were nicer and more sensitive.
- IF ONLY I could begin to change my life.
- IF ONLY SOMEBODY ELSE WOULD COME ALONG AND STRAIGHTEN MY LIFE OUT FOR ME.

The IF ONLYS usually accompany certain unrealistic masks that we wear. Those masks not only deny us the contentment in life that we deserve but they also keep us from having fulfilling and lasting relationships. Learning to grow closer means to examine these masks.

Mask #1: Macho Max

Max looks and acts tough. Trouble seems to find him wherever he goes. Max is thirty-two years old and divorced. There are very few people who can say they really know him. That's because Max won't take off his mask.

Whenever Max is in a group he is the loudest one there. Six feet, four inches tall, weighing 275 pounds, he usually does not find people resistant to his dominating ways. Max prides himself on not being a "mushy" type of guy.

"I don't run around in ballet slippers, sniffing the roses," he guffawed at his high school reunion. "And I don't live with my nose stuck in a bunch of highfalutin ideals. I'm out in the world making a buck!"

Max's mask was to appear tough. His IF ONLY was, "IF ONLY this weren't such a tough world." Affecting the appearance of being tough gave him a sense of power, so he wore this mask in order to keep himself from getting hurt in a world he perceived as tough and hard.

In reality, Max was really a sensitive man, which he feared was the same as being weak. Since weakness was something to be avoided like the plague in Max's eyes, he simply could not afford to allow the slightest movement, sound, or expression to come from him that was not machismo or overbearing. He denied his fears of weakness, and by doing so cut himself off from closeness to others and companionate love.

Outwardly, Max succeeded with the ladies because he almost parodied the western movie hero who rides into town, steely-eyed and fearless, speaking few words but appearing tough and smart. Max may have looked like the hero in a movie but he was no hero, least of all to himself. He did not want a close relationship because he was afraid of becoming dependent. Intimacy was something he actually ran from. "Anytime a woman wants to talk serious, I know I'm in for trouble," he said. "I made that mistake once and I sure don't want to make it again."

After being arrested for drunk driving, Max was heavily fined. At his request, he was sentenced to an alcohol-abuse treatment center. He figured that would be better than jail or a work sentence. Little did he know what lay ahead of him. Many of the dedicated staff at the center were Christians who prayed continually for the patients. The group sessions were particularly difficult for Max at first. He wanted to play his tough-guy role, but the group always interfered. He struggled with his "IF ONLY the world weren't so tough and cruel," and felt helpless at the idea of letting his mask crack.

One day one of the women in the group told him, "Max, you'd be so much more attractive if you acted more natural." These words got through to him. "Natural?" he asked. "You mean just ordinarylike?"

"Yes, ordinarylike," the woman responded. "You'd be nice that way. But now I think you're a real pill."

Max told me his real rehabilitation began when he realized he wouldn't be trampled on if he gave up his tough, macho image. "I guess I knew deep inside that I acted like a real pill, but I didn't know what else to do. I made a mess out of everything I ever did, including my marriage. Being tough was my way of not thinking about it."

In order for Max to experience warm and rewarding relationships, he had to take off his mask. He learned the world was not as cruel and tough as he imagined it to be. He found out that we create our own world through our beliefs, thoughts, and attitudes. He had *told* himself life was cruel and the world was awful, so he believed it. Now he taught himself new beliefs according to what God was revealing to him.

Your IF ONLYs carry the lie that you have no control over your situation. Max realized this when he started spending time studying the Word of God and attending Bible-study classes. He was amazed at how good he felt when he gave his life over to God. "I thought it was a joke before, but now I understand what 'born again' means. When I said yes to Jesus, that's how I felt. I still feel like a brand-new person, born all over again." He smiled broadly. "Everything looks better when you can see through the eyes of God. People look better—even I look better to myself." His mask had fallen.

Once Max had taken off his macho mask, he was open and vulnerable to others. He discovered, to his delight, that people liked him and he liked them in return. In time he developed a warm and caring relationship with a woman he told me he was falling in love with. He smiled and said, "If she hadn't told me to my face one day at the treatment center that I was a pill, I'd probably still be one."

Mask #2: Sweet Sue

Sweet Sue is one of the nicest people you'll ever meet. Everything about her is nice. Her dog is nice, her teapot is nice, her purse is nice, her hair is nice, her windowsills are nice—she's just plain nice. If you went into her house you would find every room nice. The bathroom would be nice with little flowers at the edge of the sink and a fluffy rug on the floor. Her car is nice. She has special covers on the front seats and a Bible verse on the dashboard. Sue rarely meets with disapproval. How could anyone find fault with such a nice person?

Sue never laughs too hard or too loud. She is friendly but never too friendly. She is kind but never ingratiating. She is intelligent but never brilliant. How could you help but love a girl like Sue?

Actually, the truth of the matter is, it's very difficult to love Sue. Those who have tried have gone away feeling confused. Sue is so sweet and so nonthreatening in her ways that you might think she would be sought after, especially by men who are looking for a sweet, submissive wife. But Sue's mask was just that—a mask. Sweet Sue's IF ONLY was, "IF ONLY the rest of the world could be as righteous as I am."

Sweet Sue was a mask that Sue had learned to wear because it made her feel superior to others. In the book I coauthored with Dr. William Backus, *Why Do I Do What I Don't Want to Do?* we talk about the sin of pride, and this includes the pride of superiority. We explain that superiority pride says, "I must try even harder to be perfect so that nobody will ever find fault with me." We show that superiority pride is really a cover-up for shyness, nervousness, and low self-esteem.[1]

Sweet Sue isn't close to anyone, even though her circle of acquaintances may be wide. She can look out at a troubled world and exclaim quietly to herself, "Thank God *I'm* not one of *them.*" Sweet Sue doesn't have compassion for others.

Sweet Sue makes a poor friend and you will always be a little frustrated with her, wondering where you went wrong.

This is how you can tell a Sweet Sue: (1) When you spend time with her or him and feel bad about yourself afterward, chances are you're responding to her attitudes of superiority. (2) You think you are unworthy of her friendship because you don't really feel you're good enough for her. (3) You have doubts about your faith in God, and you wonder why you aren't a better person. Sweet Sue gives the unspoken message that she has something exclusive in God which leaves you out.

Sue came to me because she wanted help in losing weight. She told me her appetite was out of control and she was desperate. Only after I could show Sue her unrealistic demands for perfection could we begin to understand and work through her compulsive eating patterns. Eating was her only solace in a world she perceived of as imperfect, unjust, and unrighteous. It would be a careful, step-by-step process to help Sue drop her mask.

One day, when she had finished telling me about a food binge the night before, I asked her to describe the earlier part of her day to me. "Oh, nothing unusual," she said. "I'm always uncomfortable at work." I questioned that statement. "Well, there's this guy—his name is Clayton. I really like him, and I think he likes me. I'm just so nervous around him. I feel as if he can see right through me. I've always been that way with guys. I get so embarrassed, I blush and turn crimson around them. I want them to like me, but I hate the emotional agonies I go through."

Sue didn't have a clear image of herself as a lovable person. She hadn't spent time preparing for a companionate love relationship at all. She still had a preadolescent awareness of the opposite sex, whom she viewed with external values. In order for Sue to take off her mask, she would have to tell herself that a fear of making mistakes need not run her life any longer. It took her a long time to realize that the world would not fall apart if she made a mistake.

Her IF ONLY had to go. She had to realize that nobody is better than anybody else. Sweet Sue was *not* sweeter than the rest of the world.

One day at lunchtime Clayton approached Sue and invited her to lunch. Sue told me her heart flopped around inside her chest like a "fish out of water." She turned red and could hardly look him in the eye, but she accepted. The experience proved to be almost pleasant, after she calmed down. For the next eight days she did not overeat—in fact, she hardly ate at all.

I was concerned about what would happen if Clayton proved to have some fault or appeared to be imperfect in any way. Sweet Sue might end the relationship before it began.

The Release Click I told you about earlier happened for Sue when she received a traffic ticket for driving sixty-five miles an hour in a fifty-five-mile-an-hour speed zone. We were able to talk about this and reveal that her feelings of superiority were irrational and deceiving. She was not superior. People make mistakes, including Sue!

"Do you think there's hope for me?" she asked. "Will I allow myself to love and be loved?"

With the mask gone, Sue could see herself as imperfect but blessed. She could see herself as a person not so unlike the rest of us.

Mask #3: Self-Sufficient Sam

Self-Sufficient Sam is a person who needs approval and seeks it through achievement. It is possible to be a very accomplished person and not be at all neurotic, but when a mask of any kind is worn, we are cheating ourselves out of happiness and closeness to others. Self-Sufficient Sam's mask is recognizable by his infatuation with achievement and success. The mere appearance of achievement is important to Sam. He is a person who looks for easy ways to the top, for the fastest way to make money or get ahead. He enjoys just being around success. It gives him a feeling of superiority and accomplishment, whether he's accomplished anything or not. His IF ONLY is, "IF ONLY I could make it to the top quickly, then I'd be happy."

Studies of the peptic ulcer, an erosion of the lining of the stomach and commonly of the duodenal portion of the intestines, show that there is an "ulcer type." Most researchers in the field of psychosomatic medicine agree in defining the ulcer-type person as aggressive, self-sufficient, and hard-driving. These are only the superficial or outward characteristics. Inwardly this person denies and detests the thought that he may have dependency needs. He insists on being self-sufficient and denies his hunger for love and caring, as well as his need for being dependent. In this way he's a lot like Macho Max. He accepts being dependent only if he is ill or hospitalized with his ulcer. At these times he allows himself to lie back and play the "you take care of me" role which he denies he likes or needs.

What Self-Sufficient Sam doesn't realize is that dependency doesn't have to be a total way of life. It can be faced and accepted in ways far more beneficial than getting a peptic ulcer or some other physical illness.

Achievement is important in the development of a healthy and happy life, just as companionate love is important. When achievement becomes a *need* and one's identity is paired with it, we are clearly engaging in behavior that masks our true selves.

Perhaps to the achiever, being dependent means the same as being helpless, and helplessness can be interpreted as being unloved.

Self-Sufficient Sam refuses to allow his feelings of dependency to surface and therefore never experiences the security and peace he craves because achievements aren't, in themselves, enough for a well-rounded life. His relationships suffer because he sees people as objects to further his goals. He is the direct opposite of the "Loveaholic" discussed in my book *Staying Happy in an Unhappy World*. The Loveaholic craves love and attention to feel worthwhile, but the Self-Sufficient Sams of the world crave achievement to feel they have a right to exist.

It is the most natural thing in the world for us to turn to God and relinquish our rights to ourselves by giving our dreams and goals to Him. The masks disappear when we allow our minds to be washed clean by the Spirit of God. If we push ourselves too hard in any field (including ministry and helping others), we are capable of losing out on the joy of having our needs for love met. Self-Sufficient Sam, striving and ever pressured to go onward and upward, can miss out on the rewards of being loved and nurtured on a level of stability, mutual respect, and trust. He also misses out on knowing God as his sufficiency. I've known Self-Sufficient Sams, and though they are usually outgoing, friendly, and likable, they are always behind a mask, and anybody wearing a mask is not able to be close to others.

One Self-Sufficient Sam, who was a well-known television and radio personality, had a particular problem with fear of dependency. It was hard for him to realize that dependency needs are okay. We spent long hours discussing how he could be a productive, accomplished person and still experience the carefree joy of being loved and cared for. His crumbling marriage was saved, but not until Sam learned to accept himself and others apart from his career.

Self-Sufficient Sam has to learn:

1. Being his own close friend is not only possible but necessary. If he can begin to nurture and support himself on a level beyond the external, he can receive such nurturing from others.

2. The key to freedom begins with his friendship with God. Jesus said, "Greater love has no one than this, that one lay down his life for his friends" (John 15:13 NAS). Self-Sufficient Sam can respond by laying down his mask for Him.

When we take off our masks, we are able to see ourselves for what we are, and we are then forced to accept or reject what we see. Change and growth start here. Since God always sees us in the light of truth and doesn't reject us, we are not as horrible as we may think. In accepting the friendship He offers us, we can lose nothing but gain everything.

Mask #4: Hilarious Hannah

Hilarious Hannah appears happy at all times and always wants to appear capable of handling life's troubles. If you know someone who wears the Hilarious Hannah mask, you usually feel uncomfortable in his or her presence. You compare yourself with him and wonder why you aren't as "together" and happy as he is.

Hilarious Hannah doesn't seem to have a worry in the world. You ask, "How are you?" and Hannah answers, "Great, terrific, wonderful, praise the Lord!" You feel obliged to answer in like manner. "Oh, I'm doing great too—just terrific, on top of the world." When you leave Hannah you have a headache the size of New Jersey from the stress of keeping your mask on.

We put on the Hilarious Hannah mask to deny our own fears and inadequacies. It is as if we believe a mask can actually take the place of such hard-earned characteristics as strength, courage, and wisdom. Hilarious Hannah's IF ONLY is, "IF ONLY people didn't expect me to be perfect, I would dare to be myself."

An ex-minister of a large denomination told me, "My wife and I hadn't been getting along for two years, but I never told anyone. I couldn't. People thought we were the perfect couple. I was the minister of a growing church and I just kept pushing our personal problems aside. It got worse and worse. She began to hate me, and finally she started going out with another man. The whole time we were smiling and looking like the ideal couple at church. Can you imagine? It blew up like a bomb in my face, of course, when she asked for a divorce. Everything fell apart. I lost my church, my kids, everything. She remarried after the divorce, so my kids got a new home and a new dad and I became an outsider who visits twice a month. I know we could have been helped if we had just been honest earlier and admitted we had problems. I was too proud." He wore the Hilarious Hannah mask while his home crumbled around his feet.

I wish that this story was not a common one, but it is. We feel we *must* wear masks because if people found out what we were *really* like, we would not be acceptable. We think we would be outcasts if anyone knew about our hurts and deficiencies. If that were true, we would be living in a world of 100 percent unacceptable people. Thank God, Jesus died on the cross for all of us unacceptable people, giving us the right to turn over our lives to Him and become acceptable both in his eyes and in our own eyes.

I can identify with the Hilarious Hannah mask. I used to believe the only way to be accepted in my Christian circle was to be and look like everyone else, and never, *ever* admit to problems. It was difficult for me to reconcile the faults I had with the picture of the ideal Christian I thought I was supposed to be, or at least appear to be. It took a while before I learned that "ideal" isn't appearance—it is *being*. I needed to identify what *happy* really meant, what it looked like and what it felt like. I learned this through growing closer to Jesus.

Sometimes happy on the inside does not look happy on the outside. If we were all superficial pictures of people rather than *being* the people we are, we could strike any theatrical pose and people might accept these images as our real selves. We could never afford to be close to anyone, though, because sooner or later it would have to be known that our masks and our selves were different.

There has to be at least one place in the world where we can be our real selves. These "real selves" constitute many attributes, characteristics, moods, feelings, and emotions. We treat ourselves cruelly when we do not allow ourselves the right to our feelings. Masks keep us from self-discovery and acceptance.

The Hilarious Hannah mask is a most limiting one. It takes the vastness of our human potential and turns it into a prison the size of a pinhead. How far can you go, after all, when you are confined to approvable emotions? If you have to constantly appear as if you have all the answers, you really can't go very far from home.

I can't count the times I have heard sentences like, "Marie, I'm so glad I can talk to you. You're the one person I can be myself with" or "Marie, the only place I dare to say what I'm really thinking and feeling is here in the counseling room." Because of the confidentiality and privacy of the setting and the compassion of someone who is totally on your side, the therapist's office is a refuge, a haven from what one Hilarious Hannah called "the judging eye of the world."

I remember a prayer meeting I attended once in Minneapolis. There were about twelve of us and we sat in a circle on chairs. The leader asked us to go around the circle, one by one, telling our needs and prayer requests, and then the group, in turn, prayed for these needs. One by one the people told of their hurts, doubts, wounds, and concerns for their loved ones. We prayed fervently for each person. Then it was the turn of a lady who said, "I have absolutely no needs." My mouth must have dropped open because I suddenly felt embarrassed for my own needs. There was an awkward silence and then someone asked, "Don't you have anything special you'd like us to pray for tonight?" The lady smiled placidly and answered, "No, not really. Everything is going just fine in my life." I had an urge to lend her a few of my problems. We finally encouraged her to think of some loved one or neighbor we might pray for. She was a good example of a Hilarious Hannah: no problems, doing fabulously; happy as could be.

I've thought about her many times since that evening. She must have felt like the "judging eye of the world" was ever upon her. She is divorced from her husband now, after both of them underwent severe bouts of alcoholism. Their closest friends knew nothing of their need for help. I hear that she has recovered from alcoholism and is slowly getting back on her feet. How sad that she didn't take off her mask and find a caring source of help and understanding when she most needed it.

Mask #5: Humble Harry

This mask is worn to conceal greedy ambition. "IF ONLY I appear to be humble enough, people will love me and promote me," is Humble Harry's IF ONLY. This mask is related to the Sweet Sue Mask, though different in its drives and goals. Have you ever heard statements such as, "I can take just so much and then, *boom*, I blow up"? Or how about, "I'll take a lot of abuse, but when I've had it, I've really *had* it. Just don't push me too far." These statements are usually spoken by maskwearers. Without the mask, you can assertively face the task at hand. With the mask, you're falsely humble, quiet, and patient until you can take it no more.

Look at this example of true humility: Jesus stands alone in Herod's palace. He is surrounded by a cadre of Roman guards as if He were a vicious and hardened criminal who might do violence. Herod enters the room where Jesus stands in His simple robe, beaten and battered. Only weeks earlier, Herod had ordered John's head cut off. He glares at Jesus now and asks cynically, "Who is it that you say you are?" Jesus returns his look with His steady eyes and says nothing. The great tetrarch Herod, in his long purple robe trimmed in silver, snaps at Jesus again, "Who are those whom you call your disciples?"

Jesus says nothing.

Herod becomes agitated at the silent figure before him and shouts, "It is said You can perform signs. Do something for me!"

Jesus is silent. The jeering of the priests and scribes around Him becomes louder. One priest shouts, "My lord Herod, Jesus has been corrupting the people! He calls Himself a king!"

Cruel laughter and shouts of mocking and contempt fill the air. Jesus still says nothing. The soldiers beat Him again as the crowd cheers. Then Jesus is ordered sent back to Pilate. The suffering and pain racking His body as He is dragged through Jerusalem's streets to the Antonia fortress brings no cry of defense or protest from Him. The furious crowd screams, "Crucify, crucify Him!" They jab and poke at the innocent man who now stumbles into the last hours of His life. During this mistreatment and horrible, unjust, vile behavior, the greatest Man who ever lived says nothing.

True humility is not defensive. All Humble Harrys behave defensively, using their masks as a defense against the fear that their ambitions might not be acceptable.

Humble Harry needs a defense against his or her own true feelings. He has distorted views of success: fear of it is mingled with the idea that attention and success aren't acceptable. Humble Harry might envy others who are in the limelight, but at the same time, hate them for being there.

Kathryn was a woman who wore a Humble Harry mask. She would do anything for anybody, asking little or nothing in return. She was always in the background, never in the spotlight, even though she dreamed of being in the spotlight. Her mother had always taught her that nice young ladies don't attract attention to themselves. She had conflicting notions of vanity, dreading that she might be vain, and disliking this trait in anyone else.

Kathryn was an opportunist who could not admit to her own desires. Humble, subservient, quiet, she won the hearts and trust of those she worked for. She landed a job as a governess to the children of a famous politician. She was considered one of the family and was trusted by them. In two years' time the trust disintegrated when Kathryn signed a publisher's half-million-dollar contract for a book in which she spared no juicy details of the private lives of the politician and his friends. Her account of life in Washington was seedy and destructive.

Kathryn is an extreme example of a Humble Harry. But there are variations everywhere. Humble Harry wants what you have.

Kathryn wore the Humble Harry mask to protect her from showing outwardly what she felt inwardly. It protected her from facing her fears and wants. It was a shield between her and a caring, loving world, which she saw as bad. This mask can be a dangerous one, because it deceives not only the wearer but also the unsuspecting people around them.

Taking off the Humble Harry mask is not an easy task. It was difficult for Kathryn to admit her hunger to be in a Number One spot. She craved attention and fantasized acclaim, but she could not accept those feelings. Ingrained deeply in her mind was the thought that humble people don't crave success. She defended her behavior with the lie "I only agreed to write this book because I felt it was a story that ought to be told." She continued to excuse her unethical behavior by telling herself, "Maybe the book will help somebody."

Kathryn's defenses were so solidly built in her mind that she couldn't see anything wrong with betrayal and seeking fame at the expense of others.

Taking Off the Mask

Our study of masks shows us how necessary it is for us to face our thoughts, dreams, ideas, wants, and needs without fear. When there is no one else in the room, talk to yourself about the masks you may wear.

Masks don't protect us at all when we measure our losses. Kathryn's case is a pathetic one because she saw no need to take off her mask. If she were able to look at herself through the illuminating eyes of self-acceptance, she would see that it is okay to aspire to big things; it is okay to dream of fame and glory; it is okay to hope she could accomplish something special for the world to see. These are dreams most people have in their adolescent years, and they change as we grow. They are important because they identify ourselves to ourselves.

Answer these questions:

1. What kind of person do you want others to see you as?

   _____

   _____

2. What do you think of yourself if you're not always that person?

   _____

   _____

3. What kind of person would you hate to be like?

   _____

   _____

4. Can you name a particular person you'd hate to be like?

   _____

   _____

5. Do you ever catch yourself being like that person?

   _____

6. What is one lifelong dream you've had?_____

   _____

7. Have you fulfilled any of the dreams you've had for yourself?_____

   _____

   Name as many as you can._____

   _____

8. Name three things you wouldn't want known about you.
   (A)_____
   (B)_____
   (C)_____

9. Name three things you'd want everybody to know about you.
   (A)_____
   (B)_____
   (C)_____

Answering the above questions takes time, and you may want to come back to them again as you think about getting rid of your masks. The Apostle Paul tells us in the Book of Galatians, "Live by the Spirit, and you will not gratify the desires of the sinful nature" (Galatians 5:16 NIV). When we speak of our nature, we are referring to the part of us that *chooses* worry, fear, and defense behaviors.

God's will for our lives is that we live an overcoming life, one of victory over the world's trials. In order to do this you need to look at yourself through the eyes of God. You need to know what God thinks of you and how He sees you. You learn this through His Word. Many people get their impression of God from the Hollywood interpretations of biblical stories. Others hear just one inspiring message a week on Sunday, but never throughout the week search the Word of God to understand Him and His ways better.

> The secret [of the sweet, satisfying companionship] of the Lord have they who fear—revere and worship—Him, and He will show them His covenant, and reveal to them its [deep, inner] meaning.
>
> Psalms 25:14 AMP

Jesus tells us in the fifteenth chapter of John, "You are My friends, if you keep on doing the things which I command you to do" (verse 14 AMPLIFIED). We wear masks when we run from God. We are all born to become friends of God, but not everyone chooses to be. He must be our first love. Can you dare to tear down the defenses that keep you helpless on your shabbily protected island of flesh?

The owner of a large construction company sat in my office one afternoon with tears streaming down his face. "I've never enjoyed my success," he said in an almost inaudible voice. "I've never really believed I was successful. It has seemed as if I just put one over on the world, that's all." He began to sob. "I've always been afraid to admit I'm not as good as my dad. I knew it but I couldn't admit it."

Here was someone who wore a Success mask so he could avoid his own feelings of inadequacy. He had worn his mask with defiance and almost paranoid cunning. Since he didn't believe he deserved it, he never enjoyed what his success could have given him. His home life was wretched. His wife wasn't speaking to him and his high-school-age kids were out on the street instead of in school. His mask had driven those who should have been closest to him away from him. In order to change his life, he had to make some discoveries about himself. He had to learn to say yes instead of no to himself. He had to learn to see himself as a man and not as a commodity.

There are four points that all IF ONLYS have in common:

1. Your IF ONLYS put you in the position of being helpless against your overwhelming situation.
2. Your IF ONLYS tell you that you are inadequate.
3. Your IF ONLYS tell you that success and happiness are always just out of reach.
4. Your IF ONLYS tell you that you are a failure in your personal relationships unless you wear a mask.

You can see that your IF ONLYS always lead to defeat. The following questions will help you identify your IF ONLYS and recognize the masks you wear:

1. What are you pretending to be that you are afraid you're not?_____

2. What about yourself are you hiding from?_____

_____

3. What is your worst fear?_____

_____

4. What do you wish you could remove from your past?_____

_____

5. What have your greatest joys been?_____

_____

6. What has been your greatest loss?_____

_____

7. In what ways do you receive attention and approval?_____

_____

8. What would you give to have all your dreams come true?_____

_____

9. What is the longest you've kept a close friend?

_____

10. Why would someone want to be your friend?

Taking the time to answer these questions will give you deeper insight into why you choose to wear masks. You can drop them as well as the insecurity behind them. Feelings of fear result from the way you relate to others and yourself. How you react to your own feelings of acceptance counts more than you may realize. Tell yourself the following:

- I am an okay person, regardless of my accomplishments.
- I do not have to run away from a less-than-perfect me.
- I am a person who has the power of the Holy Spirit within me to transform, renew, restore, and help me.
- God hears me and knows me. I am important to Him.
- I am worth being loved.
- I have every right to expect myself to continue on successfully in spite of past failures, mistakes, and inadequacies.
- I deserve companionate love.
- I will take off my masks because I do not need to protect myself against anything. I am completely protected and safe in the power and wisdom of God.
- I am secure in who I am.

This last statement is very important to your happiness, as we will see in the next chapter.

EIGHT

Insecurity
Is a
State of Mind

Everybody needs to feel secure. The need for security is a basic requirement for leading a happy and well-adjusted life. The word *security* comes from the Latin *securitas*, which means "freedom from care."

As we saw in the last chapter, we wear many masks in our attempts to be accepted by others. Searching for someone to love us, and at the same time being afraid of that love, is due to our insecurity, the root cause of our masks. The insecure person finds it hard to make and keep friends because he or she usually clings to friends for his feelings of self-worth. This kind of person will usually choose a friend who is stronger and, at least in his eyes, better. The emotional insecurity actually transfers to spiritual insecurity. To the insecure person, God is ineffectual in helping to meet personal needs. The insecure person constantly looks for assurance from people, not from God. Friends are *needed* passionately, rather than enjoyed fully. The insecure person has difficulty in perceiving love correctly.

Laurie was such a person. She had many friends who genuinely liked her, but Laurie didn't feel liked. She had parents who cared for her, but she did not believe they cared for her. She played the piano well but did not believe she played the piano well. When Tom, a young man she was dating, told her he was falling in love with her, she didn't believe him. She wondered what he was up to.

Insecure people do not like it when others display the very affection they so much want and need. An insecure person tries to run from companionate love. We often read of famous people who are loved by many but die feeling unloved and unwanted. An insecure person can never be famous enough or loved enough. If you try to be friends with the insecure person, you will repeatedly find yourself reinforcing your good intentions. You may even become subservient and ingratiating in your efforts to make your insecure friend feel secure, but your efforts are never quite convincing enough.

Security Begins in Your Mind

Emotional security surpasses any amount of situational security. It begins in the way you *think*. It is your inner resource, which you draw upon in times of stress and need. Everybody experiences some emotional insecurity now and then. Rejection and inconsistency give us feelings of insecurity. The child is made to feel insecure by domineering parents or overly critical ones. Negativism causes feelings of insecurity as well. If you are compared unfavorably with others, you will feel insecure about yourself and your abilities.

The danger of these feelings lies in our tendency to transfer our emotional insecurity to all of our relationships. Our insecurity tells us we are not acceptable. Acceptance by others is always such hard work, and hardly worth the effort because to the insecure person, nothing good seems to last long.

The Apostle Paul had a problem with self-acceptance. He had intense feelings of guilt over taking part in the stoning of Stephen as well as his cruel persecution of the Christians when he was a nonbeliever. He also didn't have the greatest social life. He was not a favorite in any camp because the Jews considered him a traitor and the Christians didn't trust him. Paul had reason to doubt himself and to feel insecure in who he was. There was only one way that Paul could overcome his past and his feelings of self-loathing. It is this that he passes on to us when he informs us we are new creatures in Christ (2 Corinthians 5:17). Paul had to learn that he was now a new person filled with the Holy Spirit of God. He was no longer his own person, limited to his old resources. Paul teaches us his secret of overcoming insecurity in these wonderful words:

> I am crucified with Christ: nevertheless I live; yet not I, but Christ liveth in me: and the life which I now live in the flesh I live by the faith of the Son of God, who loved me, and gave himself for me.
>
> Galatians 2:20

There are three kinds of security:

1. *Inner Security* in who we are—a sense of our own value and importance
2. *Situational Security,* when the situation we are currently in poses no threat to our well-being
3. *Social Security,* when we feel at peace and are content with the people to whom we are committed

Most of us will experience threats to our security many times in our lives. It may be threatening to you when a friend talks fondly about another friend. You worry that he or she might abandon you for that other person. It may be threatening when someone you love spends a lot of time with someone else or away from you. When you fail an exam, lose your wallet, make a bad financial decision, you feel insecure. Even being in love can give you feelings of insecurity out of fear of losing that love. These situations are threatening unless we develop Growing Closer strategies to help maintain assurance of our value in all situations.

Assurance in Insecure Situations

In 1978 my children and I stayed in a village of Zapotec Indians in Oaxaca, Mexico. We were visiting our friends Dave and Jan Persons, Wycliff missionaries. These two dedicated people have given many years of their lives to the Zapotec people, a minority of minorities. I observed firsthand the long hours and endless labor Jan and Dave freely gave to the Zapotec people. Jan could be awakened at any hour of the day or night to administer medical aid to an Indian family, and Dave was up all hours of the night working by candlelight on his translation of the New Testament Book of Mark. First the Persons had to learn the Zapotec language themselves by living with the people, because the language is not recorded. Then they had to learn and devise a way to put the language in writing. Next, the Zapotec people would have to learn to read. Finally, Dave would translate the New Testament into the Zapotec language so that the Word of God would be available to these people who still lived as their ancestors had lived hundreds of years ago.

The Zapotec Indians were unlike the African tribal people I had met. The Zapotec Indians were not friendly, nor were they eager to welcome these strange white people into their primitive society. Jan and Dave lived as outsiders in their village. In all their years with the Zapotec Indians, Jan had not formed one true friendship among the women. Though she was a miracle worker with her medicines, she was viewed with suspicion. Dave's translator-helper was a friend only in the sense that they worked together.

"Do you ever feel insecure?" I asked Jan.

She said, "Somehow God gives us the grace to go on, but if it weren't for our friends in the other villages, we couldn't make it. I think I'd go bonkers. Even though I've wanted to be a missionary all my life and most of the time I enjoy our work, I get lonely very quickly. We meet with other missionaries as often as we can. Our fellowship is wonderful and rewarding." Jan found a positive solution.

Another young woman named Zinna did not make such choices. She lives with her parents, four brothers, and three younger sisters in a tiny, overcrowded house. The family fights constantly and Zinna says there is no place for her to go for privacy and quiet. She feels insecure, but rather than seek outside friendships to build her self-esteem and sense of value, she stays home, where she is miserable. Zinna is twenty-four years old and could very well get an apartment of her own, where she could invite friends over and take charge of her life in a positive manner. She chooses to remain in unhappy circumstances.

My own experience tells me that just because we have had to face some difficult experiences in the past does not mean we are prepared to face them if they come around again. My daughters and I experienced mixed feelings of enthusiasm and insecurity when we moved from Minnesota to California six years ago. We turned to each other for emotional support and talked openly about our feelings. Christa, who was ten years old, was especially apprehensive about leaving her school friends. Liza, at nine, worried if any of the other girls in her new class would be wearing glasses.

We have moved twice since then, each move only a few miles apart, and the last one just six months ago. I was surprised to discover the same feelings of insecurity I felt when we first moved to the West Coast. I should have been so happy. Finally, a home of our own! No more rentals! But I felt frightened and depressed. Christa and Liza had the same feelings. We talked about what was going on inside us. Did buying our own home mean that we would permanently be a threesome? There was hardly room for anyone else in our little house. Did it mean we weren't on hold any longer, waiting for a prince to come along and rescue us? There were many things I had to face. I felt overwhelmed. A house of my own made the shock of being a single parent very real to me all over again.

Who would fix the plumbing, pay the mortgage, lay the tile, fix the garage door? On the "happy" first night in our new home, I cried myself to sleep.

Christa, Liza, and I talked each other into better attitudes by allowing ourselves the right to feel bad. I thanked God for daughters who have grown into my dearest friends. We love our home now and have grown closer to each other and to God than we've ever been.

Our relationship is one that allows us the privilege of expressing feelings without expecting advice. I've made many mistakes and it hasn't been rosy, but I have risen above treating love as a system of reward and punishment. I don't teach my children that they have to meet my demands in order for me to love them. They don't have to be good to receive my love. It is just *there* and theirs. Now, much to my joy, their love for each other and for me is the same: unconditional.

The Need for Approval Makes You Lonely

Some people have a greater need for approval than others. Someone with a great need for approval might say, "I never hesitate to go out of my way to help someone in trouble"; "I can't say I have ever disliked anybody"; I always try to practice what I preach"; "I'm nice to everybody whether they are nice to me or not." All of these statements are socially approved claims. A person with a high need for approval will give the socially desirable response.

People with approval needs will conform easier than others and will not show overt hostility toward people who insult or hurt them. They are less likely to use profane language and are people who work hard to get others to like them. This behavior is similar to the behavior of the person who is insecure. The motive is, "I must prove myself by being good and doing good."

It is interesting to note that the same people who hunger for social approval are often isolated people whom others describe as loners. They spend most of their time alone and do not go out of their way to make friends.

Connie was an insecure person before coming into therapy. She said she could not trust anyone, nor did she really want to be close to anyone because she was afraid of what might happen to her. "People hurt me all the time," she said. "I am tired of being hurt. I'm twenty-nine years old and still not married. My parents have disowned me and my sister hates me. Whom can I trust?"

Connie's insecurity, anger, and alienation caused her intense pain. She wanted friends and she really was a person who craved approval. Ironically, this very craving was what isolated her. She believed every lie she told herself. Connie needed to learn how to open herself up to others, but it was difficult. She was afraid she would be rejected. Connie had been hurt in the past and saw herself as unlovable. Companionate love seemed like a complete impossibility to her. She needed to drop the old way of looking at herself. I told her, "Connie, look at who you are *today* instead of who you were yesterday." The Release Click happened. She realized that she treated the people in her present as if they were the same ones in her past. In time she could accept the fact that every relationship carried a possible risk of rejection. Closeness would be worth that risk. With this new awareness, opening up wasn't so frightening.

Opening Up

Opening yourself up to others is a skill. You do it with understanding and control. The first step is to dare to disclose positive information about yourself. Self-disclosure means that you are the manager of the impression you make on others. Allow your true self to be known to at least one significant other. You can begin by telling someone simple things about yourself that are, though seemingly unimportant, special to you.

Psychologist Sidney Jourard believes that only through self-disclosure can we achieve self-discovery and self-knowledge. He says:

> Through my self-disclosure, I let others know my soul. They can know it, really know it, only as I make it known. In fact, I'm beginning to suspect that I can't know *my own soul* except as I disclose it. I suspect that I will know myself "for real" at the exact moment that I have succeeded in making it known through my disclosure to another person.[1]

This does not mean that you need to go around pouring out your soul to anybody you can get your hands on. Christians often make this mistake. We think that because we are Christians we automatically understand and appreciate one another perfectly. I have seen this happen in group meetings when virtual strangers will confess their deepest secrets and confide their most private thoughts and experiences.

Tammy, a twenty-one-year-old college student, was hurt in this way because she tried to be open and self-disclosing, but not with skill. She did it with free abandon instead of control. She was at a prayer meeting and poured out her heart to the lady next to her. Before long her story was known throughout the group, and Tammy felt humiliated and ashamed that she had confided in the woman, who was not a friend at all.

Tammy's experience reminds me of one I had recently. While shopping at a store, I was making conversation with the woman behind the counter as she busied herself gathering items from the shelves and beneath the counter. I noticed her wrists were bandaged and she had difficulty using her hands. She told me she had fallen through a plate glass window and her hands were in the process of healing. While we were talking, someone else entered the store who recognized me. When the clerk heard I was an author and Christian counselor, she changed her story instantly.

On and on she went about her life and its problems. Her marriage was in trouble, she hadn't been well, she was certain her husband was having an affair, and her son was on drugs. What did she have to live for? How could she possibly go on? My suspicions about her wrists had been correct. She hadn't really fallen through a plate-glass window.

I wanted to help her, but the store was not the place. I suggested she come and see me in the office, and I really hoped she would, but I didn't hear from her after that. I'm planning to go back to that store to see how she is doing, but I know that whatever good I can do will be minimal outside of a counseling setting. She needed help, but the time and place weren't appropriate to work through her struggles. I could only listen and pray for her.

Revealing your true self means to be able to talk about yourself openly and freely with the people you are closest to. In order to establish a close and meaningful relationship, you must be able to reveal your true self. Someone who is friendly, interested, and considerate is usually all that is expected of those who are not your most intimate friends. You can learn to enjoy people on a far more enriching basis when you identify the insecurity in your life and take steps to control it.

How Insecurity Affects Your Ability to Understand Others

Whether or not you are aware of it, other people influence nearly every area of your life. School, work, home, and play are all affected and influenced by others. Your boss's attitude toward your work affects your future. The grades a teacher gives you might influence your decision to further your education, as well as choosing a career. The people on your volleyball team, the members of your family, your neighbors and acquaintances, all play an influential part in your life. It is for this reason that understanding and predicting the behavior of others is important.

Take the typical science fiction story, where earth people travel to other planets to encounter strange terrains, exotic surroundings, and uncertain climates. They meet other beings, and then their entire cause becomes their attempt to predict the behavior of these strangers. Lack of knowledge about the strangers makes these predictions difficult. Some of us treat life as if we were on the strange terrain of another planet and all of the people around us were odd beings from another world, completely beyond our understanding. This attitude is bound in insecurity.

The first solution to insecurity is to know you are safe in God's care and love. Security will not automatically happen when things go right or when you feel good. You can't bring about a sense of inner peace and security by mentally subscribing to a set of positive precepts.

The Holy Spirit within you gives you a sense of well-being because it is His job to transmit to us the thoughts of God. God has provided us with a means to be free and secure in Him. He has provided a way for us to be at one with ourselves, with Him, and with others.

> Those who are led by the Spirit of God are the sons of God. For you did not receive a spirit that makes you a slave again to fear, but you received the Spirit of sonship. And by him we cry, "Abba, Father." The Spirit himself testifies with our spirit that we are God's children.
>
> Romans 8:14–16 NIV

God is open and direct with you. He doesn't manipulate. Others may, though. In the next chapter we'll learn how to recognize the manipulator, and more important, how to deal with him.

NINE

The
Manipulator

The man sitting across from me at lunch was well dressed in a tailored suit, custom-made shirt, designer tie, and gold tie pin. His smile flashed as brightly as the diamond rings on his fingers. When he moved his head his hair moved with it because every strand was sprayed in place. He smiled broadly now as he tapped his plate with his fork. "You ask me what makes me happy. Well, let me tell you the secret of my success, Marie. . . ." He took a breath to emphasize the importance of what he was about to say.

"One of my best secrets is this: Every time you meet someone new, ask yourself two questions—does he like me and can he help me?"

He continued as though I weren't there, but the smile remained on his face. "One of the keys to success is knowledge," he said confidently. "The more you know about people the better off you are. Remember, people will change if they can gain something or avoid a loss. That's human nature." I had my notebook in hand for our interview and was writing as he spoke. He was delighted to be interviewed and had insisted on taking me to the beautiful restaurant we now sat in.

He leaned toward me now as though what he had to say would unveil the secrets of the ages. "Marie, let me tell you, I am a wise person today because I know the meaning of success. I have some basic rules in life that have worked well for me. The first one is to be interested in other people. The second is to smile. The third rule is to always remember that a person's name is the sweetest and most important sound there is. My fourth rule is to be a good listener and to always get people to talk about themselves. The fifth rule is to talk about what the other person is interested in. My sixth rule is to make other people feel important. Yes, sir, there you have it, the six rules."

His speech sounded as if it had come straight out of a leader's guide at a motivational sales meeting. What interested me was that I had asked him about *happiness,* not success. He sat across from me smiling broadly, and yet I didn't feel as if he were really looking at me.

The man then turned the conversation to the books I had written. He wanted to know how I ever found the time to write so many books, which is not exactly complimentary to the ears of a professional author. Next he turned on the flattery and my feeling during our meeting was that he was working very hard to gain my approval of him, not because of my intrinsic worth or value but because he was using his six rules.

Why was my friend using this ingratiating manner to gain my acceptance? Dr. E. E. Jones gives these three major motives for such ingratiation. They are *acquisition, protection,* and *signification.*[1] Let me explain:

Acquisition. The goal of acquisitive ingratiation is self-gain. By behaving in an ingratiating way, a person hopes to receive favorable treatment from someone. This is the kind of behavior an employee will engage in to win the favor of an employer and possibly get a raise.

Protection. The goal of protective ingratiation is to keep from getting hurt. When someone else holds the power to control your fate, you might be tempted to behave in an ingratiating way, such as the prisoner who tries to gain favor with a sadistic guard.

Signification. We try to make others like us because

their liking us makes a statement about our personal worth. If we are liked it means we are worthy and significant. We can't like or appreciate ourselves unless someone else first approves of us. The irony is that the harder we work to win the approval of another person, the less we may value it because we feel that the other person would not like us if we hadn't worked so hard at it. I think my friend in the restaurant fell into this category.

This "give to get" perspective on social interaction reflects the distorted teaching in our culture that we can manipulate the world to get our own way. There are dozens of popular books on how to bulldoze your way to popularity and success through time-proven ingratiating methods. The Manipulator thrives on these formulas.

A Manipulator is a person who can't be happy without having his or her own way. The Manipulator doesn't have rewarding relationships based on commitment and trust. He doesn't experience companionate love. The Manipulator is doomed to poor relationships and never grows closer to people because he uses people as objects and loves only what he can get from them. He agrees with statements such as these:

> The best way to handle people is to tell them what they want to hear.
> Anyone who completely trusts another person is asking for trouble.
> Everybody has a cruel and vicious side that eventually comes out.
> It's safer to be feared than to be loved.

Those last words were spoken by Niccolò Machiavelli, who lived in the sixteenth century and was well known for the use of manipulation and deceit for personal gain and political benefit. "It is far safer to be feared than loved," was the advice Machiavelli gave the Prince of Florence. Machiavelli also said, "Humility not only is of no service but is actually harmful." He spoke of people as *things* to be manipulated. To him, human beings were objects to be approached with emotional detachment. With clever calculation and planning, he could manipulate people to do whatever he wanted of them. He had no regard for morality or honesty and, in fact, endorsed lying and cheating if the end justified the means.

A Prince in a World of Frogs

A modern Machiavellian is typified as a con man, a person who endeavors to sell things to people whether they want them or not. This person believes he is a prince in a world of frogs. To become a friend to such a person is nearly impossible. His or her usual prey is members of the opposite sex. His charm works wonders in the poor, unsuspecting target's fluttering heart. Clinically the Machiavellian is an antisocial personality. This person simply does not relate to the feelings of others. He is outwardly charming and says caring words but his only thought is of himself. He is preoccupied with how to promote himself and how others will respond to his success.

The Manipulator may not always be a Machiavellian. People may engage in manipulative behaviors and not really be con artists, but they are still difficult to understand and to maintain a close relationship with. Manipulative behavior is a destructive force in any relationship. Here is an example of manipulation:

MOTHER: (*on telephone*) Hello, Jenny—this is your mother.

JENNY: Hi, Mom. How are you?

MOTHER: Oh, not so good. . . .

JENNY: What's the matter?

MOTHER: Oh, nothing really . . . it's probably just my kidneys again.

JENNY: I didn't know there was anything wrong with your kidneys.

MOTHER: I don't like to worry you, dear. It's nothing.

JENNY: Wait a minute. *What's* nothing?

MOTHER: I'll be fine, Jenny, don't you worry. I know

you're busy with your new job and all. . . .

JENNY: Mother, are you sick?

MOTHER: The doctor says I have a good chance.

JENNY: Please put Dad on the phone.
(pause)

FATHER: Hello, Jenny. When are you coming home?

JENNY: Dad, is Mom all right?

FATHER: She's sick, Jenny. Are you coming home?

JENNY: No, I'm not coming home—not until the seventeenth. What's wrong with Mom?

FATHER: She's been sick for the last two days.

JENNY: How sick?

FATHER: Sick enough. You could call, you know.

JENNY: I called three days ago. You were both fine then.

FATHER: Ever since you got that new job you're too busy for your mom and dad. Too busy to call your mom and dad or pay a visit—

JENNY: I'm sorry you don't think I call enough or see you enough, but I'm trying to make a life for myself, to build a career and become independent.

FATHER: There you go again with that smarty-pants talk.

MOTHER: *(taking phone)* Jenny, why are you upsetting your father? You know his heart isn't good.

JENNY: I'm sorry Dad is upset. Will you tell me honestly how you are, Mother?

MOTHER: How can you treat your father like that? He has given so much for you—all he wants is for you to call just once a day. Is that too much to ask?

FATHER: *(in background)* A visit home once in a while would be nice while we're still alive!

MOTHER: You're all we've got. You used to be so sweet, so loving, Jenny. Since you've become a big career person, you've changed. You're just not the same daughter anymore.

JENNY: Mother, I love you and Dad very much. I told

you I'd be home on the seventeenth for Dad's
birthday. I've made all the arrangements.

MOTHER: The seventeenth is so far away. Who knows
what could happen between now and then.

FATHER: (*taking phone*) Don't you care that your mother
isn't well? Doesn't it bother you at all that she
may need her daughter now, with her kidney
trouble?

JENNY: You haven't told me what the trouble is yet, but
I'll be home on the seventeenth and I'll find out
then. Meanwhile, I'll call you in two days and
we can talk again. I'd better go now. I love you
both.

FATHER: You'll call in two days? Is that a promise?

JENNY: You can count on it, Dad.

FATHER: Okay, but if there's no answer, just call the hos-
pital.

You can see from this dialogue that Jenny's parents were
unskilled in communicating their wants to their daughter
and were quite adept at manipulative behavior. Jenny
wasn't responding the way they wanted her to so, typical
of manipulative persons, they attacked her for being ne-
glectful. In this case, Jenny was a bad daughter because of
her career.

Manipulative behavior is used by people to get their
own way by shaming others or making them feel guilty.
This is evident in the manipulative behavior of Jenny's
parents. In an effort to shame their daughter into doing
what they wanted her to, they said things such as, "I don't
like to worry you, dear. It's nothing" and "Ever since you
got that new job, you're too busy for your mom and dad."
They also used manipulative guilt tactics: "You're all
we've got. You used to be so sweet, so loving . . . you're just
not the same daughter anymore."

You see manipulation through shame and guilt every
day in advertisements. A good example is the kind of ad-
vertisement that indicates we don't care about our loved

ones unless we feed them a certain product. "If you *really* loved your family, you would not let them live a day without *X*."

If you can make somebody feel guilty, you can usually manipulate that person to do what you want. That's the sad truth of it. Understanding this truth ought to make you wiser and more sensitive in your own behavior, as well as wiser and alert to the behavior of other people. Look at this example of a married couple: Roger has just come home from work—late again. It is after 9:00 P.M. and his wife, Penny, is sitting in the living room by herself. Roger enters and the scene goes like this:

ROGER: Hi, honey, I'm home. (*no response*) Penny? I'm home.
(*Roger enters living room and sees Penny slumped in chair*)
Penny? What's the matter?

PENNY: (*barely audible*) Hello, Roger.

ROGER: Don't be angry, Penny. I *had* to stay late. There is so much to do at work this time of year. Please understand.

PENNY: I'm not angry. I understand.

ROGER: Well, how about a kiss, then?

PENNY: (*she gives him a quick peck, deliberately missing his mouth*) Aren't you going to ask about the kids?

ROGER: Sure. How are they?

PENNY: Billy's sick and Missy fell and hit her head.

ROGER: Did you call the doctor?

PENNY: Sure I did, but I couldn't have gotten to his office if he had told me to come right over, could I? I don't have a car and *you* work day and night.

ROGER: Good heavens, are the kids all right?

PENNY: They cried for their daddy. They thought you would be home for dinner as you promised.

ROGER: That makes me feel horrible, Penny. I *had* to

work. What could I do? Didn't you explain to
them?

PENNY: And me here at home with no car, no way to get
anywhere. I couldn't even get to the doctor today.
The neighbor wasn't home to drive me. (*she starts
to cry*)

ROGER: Honey, you know we can't afford another car
yet. . . .

PENNY: I don't know when to believe you. You promise
you'll be home but just when I trust you, you disappoint me. You've been home late every night
for five days. Tonight I even made your favorite
dinner because you promised you'd be home. You
just don't care. (*sobbing*) Your family doesn't mean
anything to you.

ROGER: That's not true. I *love* you. That's why I'm working so hard—so we can buy the things we need.

PENNY: Like a car for me?

ROGER: Well (*he knows they can't afford it but feels so
guilty he can't say no*), yes—like a car for you.

PENNY: (*sobbing loudly*) Can we go out tomorrow and
look for one?

ROGER: Well, yes, honey, I suppose we could get the
credit—

PENNY: Oh, Roger, you *do* love me.

Penny's desire for a new car was legitimate. Roger's
working overtime was also a legitimate need. The trouble
was, neither Penny nor Roger knew how to communicate
their feelings or their wants in constructive ways. Penny
did not have to resort to manipulation by guilt in order to
get a car.

Your wants are important to those you care about, and
you can address yourself directly and openly without re-
sorting to tears, complaints, or other manipulative devices.
Penny and Roger did not lack love but they lacked skill in
communicating. Love without skill can become a night-

mare. Notice how much better the scene could have been played:

ROGER: Hi, honey.

PENNY: Hello, Roger. (*she greets him with a kiss*)

ROGER: I'm sorry I'm late again.

PENNY: Is there any way you could let me know in advance on the days you'll be late?

ROGER: Well, it looks as if I'll be putting in overtime every night at least for the next three weeks.

PENNY: I appreciate knowing that in advance because I can plan meals differently and arrange the kids' schedule so they can see you.

ROGER: How *are* the kids?

PENNY: One minor mishap and one slight fever. I'll give you details after you've eaten your dinner, which is in the kitchen.

ROGER: I miss you when I work such long hours.

PENNY: Roger, I feel jealous of those hours you work, but I know for now it's necessary, especially if we're to get a second car.

ROGER: Well, I hadn't planned on getting another car just yet.

PENNY: We must have one. It's important that I be able to get around on my own. It is also important for the children's sake, and for emergencies that might come up. I've made a plan for the payments, which we can go over after you've eaten.

ROGER: You've really done a lot of thinking and planning about this, haven't you?

PENNY: Yes, I have, because it's so important to me.

ROGER: Penny, if you've figured out a way we can afford it, we'll get that car. In fact, we could even go out tomorrow and look for one.

PENNY: Good.

This second scenario with Penny and Roger shows how they handled conflict to build intimacy rather than to erode it with manipulation. Penny was open and confrontive, and their interaction led to an assertive conclusion. In the prior conversation, Penny resorted to manipulation by trying to make Roger feel terrible about coming home late. When they talked about their feelings and wants in a non-accusing, nonmanipulative way, they avoided a major blowup, which would have led to more misunderstanding, miscommunication, and frustration.

Manipulative behavior is not usually a conscious decision or plot. Penny did not sit down and tell herself before Roger came home, "I'm going to manipulate him now by making him feel guilty so I can get a car." But because manipulative behavior is not deliberately planned does not make it any less painful or any more acceptable.

It is difficult for the manipulative person to take responsibility for the negative consequences of his or her actions. The manipulative person cannot recognize the rights of others and can't understand when someone objects to being manipulated. Words such as "Beloved, love one another" and "Love others as yourself" speak to the manipulator of *getting*, not *giving*.

How to Put a Stop to Manipulation

We have talked about reinforcement elsewhere (*see* chapters 2 and 13). You can see how it applies to manipulation. The principle to remember is that behavior which is reinforced is usually repeated. This behavioral principle holds true for negative as well as positive behavior. For example, if you want something badly enough from somebody and you know you can get it by whining and crying, you will whine and cry until you get your own way. Your whining and crying is *reinforced* by the fact that it works in your favor. Psychologically, *reinforce* means "reward." Let me give you another example of the way we reinforce poor behavior:

Suzanne is a quiet woman and rarely gets much attention at the office. One day she comes to work with a cold. Nearly everyone who passes her desk stops to ask her how she feels. Suzanne talks about her cold and about the various cough drops and cold tablets she is taking. Even her boss pays more attention to her than on other days. It's no wonder, then, when a short time later Suzanne becomes sick again. And not long after that she shows up at work with a sprained wrist. When she has something wrong with her, she receives a lot of attention. It is reinforcing for Suzanne not to be well.

This book stresses the importance of knowing yourself and your wants and needs in order to find intimacy with others. We all need to be noticed and to feel we are necessary and important. This recognition is what we can give to one another. Becoming aware of manipulating others, and realizing when others are manipulating us, is a vital step in the journey toward intimacy.

What Kind of People Are Most Frequently Manipulated?

In the counseling office I see several personality types who are always in danger of being manipulated. The most obvious person is the one starving for attention (*see* chapter 5), an easy prey for the Manipulator. If you are desperate for approval, or if you are a person who hates to make waves or face conflict, you are a sitting duck for a Manipulator to shoot at. If you are a person who has very little respect for yourself, you can be manipulated to become the shadow or slave of someone else. The Machiavellian will con you and rob you, and the Manipulator will hurt and use you. The person who can be easily manipulated is one who is unsure of himself or herself, and one without interpersonal skills.

Every year countless people are bilked out of large amounts of money because of shrewd and calculating con artists, or Machiavellians who prey upon unskilled, naive people. The more lonely and hurting a person is, the better victim he makes.

Every year senseless crimes are committed and the victims are the starving-for-attention, unfulfilled, hurting people. Detective Lloyd Martin of the Los Angeles Police

Department said in an interview that out of four thousand pedophiles and their victims studied, not *one* of the victims came from a loving home. That's a staggering thought, isn't it? The helpless child victim who is hungry for love falls into the clutches of the child molester because he is easy prey for such vile Manipulators. A healthy sense of being loved, of being necessary, of being important, is crucial to our identity. Before going any further, stop and ask yourself these questions:

True or False:

1. I am a person who trusts everybody._____
2. I can't stand to hurt anybody's feelings._____
3. People often take advantage of me because I don't speak up for myself._____
4. I try never to disagree with people because I hate an argument._____
5. Being loved is the most important thing in the world to me. If I'm not in love, I'm totally miserable._____
6. I'll do anything so I don't have to be alone._____
7. What I want most in life is to be rich and famous._____
8. I enter every sweepstakes contest and drawing I can because one of these days I just know I'll win the jackpot._____
9. I'm waiting for Mr. Right (or Ms. Right) to come along and rescue me from futility._____
10. I know I'm destined for greatness; I just need to be discovered._____

If you answered True to three or more of the above, you're a good candidate for the devices of the Machiavellian or the Manipulator. Your unrealistic ideas of love make you an easy prey. The dream of being rich and famous or getting rich without effort is just what the Machiavellian loves to find. You may be the gullible soul willing to buy the proverbial Brooklyn Bridge. Also, if you are waiting for someone else to solve your problems, you are just what the Manipulator and the Machiavellian look for. They are just waiting to be the savior you are longing for—and they'll take what they can, saving nothing for you.

Now ask yourself these questions to see if you can recognize your own manipulating behaviors:

True or False:

1. I believe in always being one step ahead of the other guy so he doesn't run me over._____
2. If I'm going to be successful, I've got to make every opportunity count._____
3. I agree with W. C. Fields: "Never give a sucker an even break."_____
4. All people are alike—they are only out for themselves._____
5. I'll never let anyone take advantage of me again._
6. I hate making mistakes and try not to admit it when I do._____
7. I have to get my own way in order to feel good about myself._____
8. I never give another person the right to disagree with me._____
9. I must defend myself when I make a mistake._____

If you answered True to three or more of the above, you are a person who manipulates. You may be going along in life thinking you're a pretty terrific person, but then something happens: an argument you refuse to lose, or somebody has something you want. You slide into high-gear manipulating.

Manipulators are never really close to people because they usually choose friends for what they can get out of them. They even marry for the same reason. Though not as hard-core as the Machiavellian, the Manipulator nevertheless is deceived into thinking his or her attitudes and behavior are perfectly normal. They aren't.

The Manipulator is not aware of his own needs and simply plunges ahead with the misbelief that power would give him gain and admiration. If the Manipulator is a man, he will have no close relationships, especially with other men. He is utterly dependent on the opinions of others. He wants praise and acclaim desperately, but because he is selfishly uncaring, the very thing he wants eludes him. When our conscience becomes dull, our sensitivity to the needs of others is extinguished. Then we can exploit others without compunction.

The Manipulator is a person who generally puts selfish desires first, while remaining unaware of his own needs. He wonders why he can't grow closer to people. He is trapped in his own selfishness. It resembles a disease, and the only cure is the living awareness of God and who we are in relation to Him. That awareness begins with choice. Gently and slowly, take time now to tell yourself:

- I choose to accept myself and others equally as the Lord sees us.
- I can give myself the right to be wrong occasionally. I do not have to be right in all things.
- Other people are just as valuable as I am. I can relate to others for no other reason than to relate.
- I can dare to disagree with others in an assertive, nonmanipulative way.
- I do not *crave* love and attention; I choose to learn more about myself and God so He can guide me in all I do.
- People are not objects. I gain in life because God prospers me. I belong to *Him.* My future is *His.* I bow my knee to Him.
- I choose to be understanding and patient. People need not serve my needs and wants.
- No one rescues me. I rescue myself through the power of the Holy Spirit.
- I choose to concentrate on the sweet, giving heart of Jesus.
- My goal is not to think more highly of myself than I

ought to think, because that is not sound judgment.

- I am a loving, giving person who can dare to be less than the greatest, the best, or the tops. Jesus is the One who defines my success.
- I am a person who chooses to be giving and compassionate instead of fearful or taking in my relationships.

Now that we recognize some of the obstacles to Growing Closer, let's look at ways to create intimacy with those we love.

PART THREE

Strategies
for
Growing Closer

TEN

When a Good Relationship Goes Bad

We have looked at what intimacy is. We have looked at the obstacles to it. Now we are going to look at how to create intimacy by finding out why relationships go bad.

You Know You Have Formed a Poor Relationship If:

- You have a feeling of irritability, coupled with restlessness and discontent, when with the other person.
- You feel guilty or unclean when with the person.
- You are on guard, watching what you say and do, knowing you could meet with disapproval.
- You feel you must act a certain way to be acceptable, even if it is dishonest.
- You are tempted to do things you would not ordinarily do if you could help it.
- You are overtaken by his or her controlling personality and find yourself doing what he wants to do and being the person he or she insists you be.
- The relationship leaves you drained.
- You are verbally abused, perhaps even in a joking manner.
- You set aside your own goals, dreams, and preferences for the wants and needs of another, living solely for his or her supposed happiness.
- You do not share a common love for the Lord Jesus.

Usually, when you encounter something you don't like, your first response is to categorize it. By "categorize" I mean we decide whether it is good or bad. Then we respond accordingly. If we judge a thing as bad, we will respond with a set of programmed negatives. Let me give you an example:

George yells at Shirley. Shirley recoils defensively, judging his behavior as hostile and cruel. Since her judgment is negative, her response is negative. Typically, Shirley's response to hostility has been to recoil at George's behavior in a childlike, helpless stance.

Her immediate urge is to change things instead of trying to understand them. Shirley wants George to stop yelling, so she tries to shut him out by covering her ears and pressing her eyes shut. If Shirley were another man at whom George was venting his hostility, the man might clench his fists and pop him in the face. This would be his way of changing George's behavior. It would be his response to stop something which he judged as bad. This is not pausing to understand but responding in an already programmed, preexperienced, negative response.

We look for immediate solutions and don't pause to discover what caused the conflict. Many people suffering from anxiety take tranquilizers without making much of an investment in understanding themselves and their emotions.

Some people treat their most precious relationships in the same way they would operate a business. I knew one man who sent neatly typed memos to his family. Each child was expected to initial the memo after carefully reading it. This same man had the house rules typed up and put into booklet form. He distributed one copy to each family member. If there was an infraction of a rule, he would have that child memorize an article on goal setting, decision making, or how to be more responsible. He was especially intolerant of lateness, and often had temper outbursts which terrified the family when anyone ever had the impertinence to keep him waiting.

What could this man do to maintain order in his home? He couldn't very well fire his children for insubordination. He couldn't dock his wife's pay (although he tried that once by telling her because she left the furnace running at 72 degrees all day when nobody was home, he would dock her house allowance. It drew such a torrent of protest, including tears and feigned illness, that he withdrew his penalty).

When his son received a memo from him one day with "From the Office of the President" at the top, that was the last straw. The angry teenager objected, but his father argued, "How can you be so ungrateful? I give you a good home and you have everything you need. Is it too much to want to have a little order around here?"

The son clammed up, realizing it was a mistake to confront his father. The tirade continued a while longer, as the father accused the son of not appreciating all he had given him. He raved on about how the whole family was taking advantage of him. He was out slaving away, working all day, while the rest of them were simply finding ways to spend his money. Though hurt, angry, and feeling misjudged the son still chose to say nothing. Neither father nor son opened any channels of mutual understanding. The walls remained and their relationship crumpled, like the discarded office memos.

The father was not the sort of person who would seek counseling because he really didn't see that he had any problems. He believed the problem was his children, and his wife didn't care about his feelings. The mother was the one who came to me for help.

"I'm in the middle and I can't take it," she told me tearfully. "He treats me as though everything that goes wrong is my fault. He can't relate to the kids. I feel sorry for them because they're really good boys and he can't see that."

Before a satisfying solution could be discovered, each family member needed to understand more about themselves and one another.

When conflicts arise:

1. Avoid categorizing the other person's behavior because it glues you into immobility when you pass sentence.
2. Neither change nor finding a solution is *the* most important goal in conflict. Communicating is most important.
3. In the process of mutual understanding, change and solutions are discovered.

Two key words in conflict are *explore* and *understand*. In our goal-setting society, where decision making and solution seeking are primary aims, we fail to stop to discover the source of our feelings as well as the source of another person's feelings. Without understanding what causes conflict, the solution may be only temporary. The symptoms have been treated but the cause has gone untreated.

In order to explore and understand one another, we must drop categorizing and sentencing. Absolutely *no* finalized statement about a person's character is allowed in the exploring process. Here are some examples:

"I can tell you're upset. What can I do to help you feel better?" (NOT, "You're always upset about *something*. What is it this time?")

"Is there something you want that you're not getting right now?" (NOT, "Oh, no, you're going to be a grouch again.")

"You're very quiet. Are you feeling distant?" (NOT, "What's *wrong*? Is something *wrong*? There's always something *wrong*.")

"My irritability must give you feelings of being shut out. I don't want to do that." (NOT, "I have a right to express my feelings. I express my feelings the way I want to.")

"When we disagree, let's take the time to understand why each of us has the feelings we have. Maybe then we can come to an agreement that will be mutually satisfactory." (NOT, "*You* are always the one who starts the fights.")

When a good relationship goes bad, there are so many

factors at work that it takes the investment of your time, energy, and awareness to make the discoveries that are necessary for rebuilding mutual happiness.

Three causes for a breakdown in communication and the demise of a relationship are:

1. One or both persons do not let the other know his or her feelings are important and understood.
2. One or both persons regard the other's feelings as less important than getting one's own way, meeting a certain standard, saving face, appearing to do the right thing, or achieving gain.
3. One or both partners do not want to explore the depths of each other's feelings. They are inhibited about discussing feelings and say they want "peace in the relationship" (which means suppressing or "stuffing" feelings, something nobody can do successfully).

Let's look at some examples of relationships that once were good but now have gone bad. What brings a relationship to its demise? The following are three of the worst culprits:

Indifference

When two partners withdraw emotionally from a relationship, what's left is communication on a shallow basis. The daily routine is their only common ground. People in this kind of relationship rarely seek counseling because they don't think anything is wrong. They have settled for safety above their happiness. But then one day a shocking event might take place. One of the partners discovers what it is like to have someone outside the marriage *care* about his or her feelings. This is the case when a man or a woman will come in for therapy, utterly devastated because a marriage partner of twenty-five years has found another love.

"Is it his midlife crisis?" a woman named Agatha asked me.

"I thought we always got along so well. We hardly ever

fought. I have kept his house, ironed his shirts, scrubbed his floors, cooked his meals, raised his children—and now, he finds himself another woman. I can't believe it. How could he do this to me?"

What Agatha didn't realize was that her husband could have hired someone to do all of the things she named, in fact, someone who spoke a foreign language and one he could hardly communicate with other than to discuss daily matters and give instructions for the daily household tasks.

A perfect relationship is not one where two people exist dispassionately together, with few lows and few highs. A perfect home is not always one where the floors shine and the dishes are washed.

Two sisters named Emma and Sally have lived together for the last five years. They are both retired widows. Their conversation usually consists of their comments on some horrible thing they have read in the paper, how high prices are, or what varied infirmities they are suffering. When they are angry with one another, they simply do not talk to each other. In this way they punish each other and avoid talking about feelings. When their husbands died, they didn't share their sorrow and fears. They have never discussed their feelings for each other.

Outwardly Emma and Sally look like two nice little old ladies who are leading very peaceful lives together. The truth is, they are bitter women who punish the world and each other by withdrawing into themselves. Icy silence and noncommunication are punishers. There are no stormy arguments, but then there are no warm and open conversations, either. Some common statements by people in an indifferent relationship are:

"Whenever we talk, he always complains, so why talk at all?"

"She is so closed. It's impossible to get through to her."

"We never talk anymore. I guess we have nothing to say."

"He just isn't interested in my feelings or how I think about things."

"Maybe I really don't know her very well after all."

"I have feelings and needs and wants, but if I express them to him, I'm afraid I'll just get laughed at or ignored."

Those statements can either keep you indifferent or awaken you to learning Growing Closer strategies. Indifference is called the "opposite of love" because at least there is some passion in hate. Indifference is a devastating emotion to bring to any relationship.

There is no one who can tell you, "Now, see here, you must stop all this indifference business," and expect you to follow through. Feelings cannot be dictated. You can do nothing to help a person *want* to feel. You can't force someone to care about your feelings, just as you can't force someone to love you. You are responsible only for your own feelings and behavior, not somebody else's. The good news is that feelings can be explored, understood, and expressed. These are what to aim for when your indifference robs a relationship of joy. Communicating is what will bring two estranged people together again as friends. Saying sentences to each other that begin with "I feel," is the beginning.

Avoiding Consequences

Another destructive behavior in any relationship is not facing the fact that negative words and actions bring consequences. You may start a fight during which you hurt yourself and somebody else. If you ignore or avoid facing the fact that there are bound to be negative consequences, the relationship suffers.

You are responsible for the things you say and do. A relationship suffers when words are spoken out of irresponsibility and carelessness. Cruel and accusing words hurt, no matter how tough we seem. Putting the blame on another person, and disregarding that other person's feelings, are behaviors that destroy closeness. Do not avoid facing the consequences of your thoughtless behavior. If you mistreat someone, you are the one who loses because you separate yourself from closeness. If you lie, be ready to take the consequences when you are discovered. If you yell, accuse, call names, judge, insult, or curse a person, don't think you can get away with it without leaving serious scars, no matter how sincerely you apologize later.

The mother of an eleven-year-old boy told me, "I yell at him all the time. I can't help it. I call him names like 'bum,' 'no good,' and 'rotten kid' all the time." The consequences are the construction of a thick wall between this mother and son. The son told me, "I don't even hear her anymore. She used to be so much fun. Now I don't even like being around her."

A person who doesn't care about the consequences of his or her own behavior will say things like the following:

"Did I say that? I didn't really mean it." (The truth is, you probably did mean it at the time, and it would be better to face your feelings.)

"It wasn't *my* fault—it was *your* fault." (When you refuse to take consequences, you don't think things are ever your fault.)

"I was just in a bad mood, that's all." (Feeble excuse. We all feel bad at times.)

"I'll say what I please and do as I please. I answer to nobody." (And a happy aloneness to you.)

The Silent Treatment

I don't think I've ever seen any behavior as destructive as the silent treatment. Pat, a vivacious and bright woman, was worried about her friend Judy. She could hardly concentrate on her work. At night she slept fitfully, which made it difficult to get up in the morning. She carried herself through the day somewhat in a daze: tired, confused, and unable to concentrate. Judy, her friend of ten years, had stopped speaking to her and Pat didn't know why. They had been best friends for all those years. They had talked daily and shared all of their common interests. When Judy stopped communicating with Pat, it was seemingly without provocation. Pat would call Judy repeatedly and ask what was wrong. "Nothing," was the cold reply.

Pat never did learn what was wrong. She had no idea that Judy had felt belittled for many years because she always suspected that Pat thought she was better than Judy. Finally she decided she could take it no more, after Pat had told her not to wear a certain sweater because it didn't look good on her. Pat was oblivious to the fact that she had hurt Judy's feelings, yet Judy thought she had every right to give her the silent treatment.

"I just don't want to feel inferior anymore," Judy said. Pat, on the other hand, thought she had always been the one who did the giving in the relationship. She had tried to comply with Judy's every wish in order to keep peace, and she had thought she was a good friend to her. She was always there in times of need and now she felt lost, deeply wounded, and bitter.

If Pat and Judy had explored and discussed their feelings in order to understand each other, perhaps their friendship would not have ended the way it did. Pat would have been able to respond in a positive, open manner if Judy had told her, "I often feel inferior because of the things you say. It reminds me of when I was a child, and my older sisters used to push me around. I always felt inferior and inadequate around them."

Pat would then have had the opportunity to share in return, "I had no idea you felt that way. Tell me when I make you feel inferior so that I can be aware of my actions. I want to let you know my feelings and I want to know yours. In this way our friendship will be enriched and we will both be better people for it." This second strategy for communicating only enhances a loving relationship.

Dr. Ari Kiev gives five of the most important elements of a loving relationship.[1] I share these with you because if a relationship is to survive it needs:

1. the capacity to balance individuality and togetherness
2. the capacity to change over time
3. the capacity to escape the past
4. the capacity to express feelings
5. the capacity to listen

Check the five points. If one is missing in your close relationships, you are on shaky ground. When a person decides to leave a relationship, or worse, to withdraw himself emotionally and mentally while there physically, you have a situation where love either needs to be recaptured or *accepted as missing.* Love cannot tolerate indifference, avoidance of consequences, or the silent treatment. Feelings need to be expressed, and there is a way to do that if you don't talk yourself out of them.

ELEVEN

Don't
Talk Me Out
of My Feelings

Feelings are important and need to be heard as well as expressed. A husband and wife were arguing in my office one day. She expressed some irrational feelings: "I feel as if I'm all alone and nobody really cares!" He immediately responded, "That's not true! I care and so do a lot of other people." Rather than try to understand the feelings being expressed, the man wanted to talk her out of them. Her remark to him is worth remembering. She said, *"Don't try to talk me out of my feelings."*

We do that to one another. Rather than listening, we try to talk each other out of the way we feel. How many times have you said to somebody, "What have *you* got to be angry about? You have so much to be thankful for." Or, "Don't be upset. Everything always works out." Or, "Stop that crying this instant. Big boys don't cry."

When we respond in these ways, we not only close the channels of communication, but we also stifle growth in the other person. If you can't express your feelings in an open way, you feel misunderstood and frustrated. This leads you to either hide your feelings or deceive the other person into thinking you're feeling what you are not. I remember walking into a classroom I thought was empty at the University of Minnesota. A young man was standing in the corner, his face red and his body bent forward in anger and pain. I thought he was ill, but then he punched the wall, crying out, "She never *listens* to me!" He was painfully acting out his frustration at not being heard.

Lying is another way we talk ourselves out of feelings. "No, I *don't* feel angry. I'm just tired, that's all," is an example. Another lie is, "I didn't want to act mean. I'm just not feeling well lately." These lies are saying, "I'm afraid to tell you how I really feel. I do feel angry and I purposely acted mean because I'm hurt." Only when these feelings are faced, admitted, and talked about can a resolution be found.

Deceit brings about a cycle of guilt, more deceit, followed by guilt, followed by more deceit. If I tell a lie I will feel guilty. But then I have to tell another lie in order to cover my first lie so I'll feel guilty again. Then because I'm afraid to tell you my true feelings, I will go on deceiving you and feeling bad about myself. I won't be able to tolerate these feelings forever. How much better to allow someone to actually express his or her feelings, whether these feelings are negative, unpleasant, or what you don't want to hear. As long as the feelings are not accusing, demanding, or condemning to the other person, they need to be expressed and heard.

Expressing your feelings does not mean accusing or putting the blame on somebody else.

Admitting Mistakes Without Feeling Guilty

When we are afraid to make mistakes it is usually because we have to pay so dearly for them. When you feel free to talk about your mistakes with a friend, it is because that friend will not categorize and sentence you. When you are allowed to express your feelings without fear, you will not be tempted to lie or deceive yourself or your friend.

Suppose Johnny told his mother, "Mother, I'm late because I wasted time on the way home. Not only did I stop at Jimmy's house but I also sat down at the side of the road and watched some kids play ball." If his mother responded in a rage, calling him names and taking out the stick to punish him for being late, do you suppose the next time he would be as honest? This happens to adults all the time. We punish each other for our mistakes, so it is painful to admit them. We would rather do anything than admit our mistakes. We *categorize* each other as wrong and then we sentence each other to punishment. But then we wonder why we feel so isolated. Sometimes we don't need another person to criticize; we do it ourselves.

More than anything, I've always wanted to be a model mother, especially when my daughters were younger. I was more naive then. In those days when I got angry, I blamed it on the fact that I am part Italian. "My temper is the Italian in me," I'd say. If I became angry with my girls I would cry out to the Lord to help me overcome my Italian temper. My children were so sweet, I wanted to be the perfect model of temperance and patience for them.

One day when the girls were fighting over who was going to play with which Barbie doll, I charged into the room and plunked them both down on chairs opposite each other as a punishment. "Now sit there and be quiet," I snapped. Then I left the room and felt horrible about myself. They didn't deserve my outburst. If I was supposed to be the model mother, why didn't I lovingly enter the room and demonstrate the loving way to share a Barbie doll? What I really wanted to do was throw the thing out the window.

I was still praying about my behavior later when I suddenly felt impressed to stop repenting and look at the causes for my temper outbursts. What was I *feeling,* and why? Often the smallest thing would bother me, and other times the roof could fall in and I would calmly carry on. It didn't take me long to recognize that if I had negative thoughts such as worry and fear, and I was fretting over countless matters, I would have a short fuse with my children. Self-pity was my worst enemy.

Feelings need to be examined. I did not want to talk myself out of them. I learned that lesson and am still learning it. What messages are we giving ourselves when we feel bad? It could be self-pitying worries about bills, pressures at work, a disagreement with someone, or any number of other negatives. Recognize them. Be in control of what you think about.

I had to tell myself to *stop it* when I couldn't control my thoughts. I could see how I was agitating my whole being with such negative fears. Thoughts can dominate your actions. All behavior is the result of your thoughts, and you must be aware of this if you are going to have any degree of satisfaction in your life. Invest some time learning the following Growing Closer skills to understand how to handle negative feelings. Instead of talking yourself out of or ignoring your feelings:

1. Tell yourself that you were created to handle conflict. (Worry tells you you're a weakling in the face of trouble.)
2. Be aware of your negative thinking and allow yourself only a short amount of time to engage in it. Don't try to squelch your fears and worries, but put a limit on how much time you'll allow for worrying.
3. After your time for worrying is up, begin positive, constructive thinking about how to solve the problem that is troubling you.
4. Take steps to be good to yourself, and be aware of not *acting out* your discontent. You can be pleasant in spite of your personal troubles.
5. Nobody else should be expected to share your worries and feel the same as you do about them. Sharing them openly, without emotional manipulation, leads to understanding.
6. Nobody else should be expected to carry your worries for you—but you can be comforted.
7. Tell yourself you can handle all trials through

Christ, who gives you strength. Jesus makes weak people strong.

8. Admit your feelings and don't blame anyone else for them. You are the only one in charge of them.

Who Is to Blame?

A good relationship deteriorates when you put the blame for your unhappiness on somebody else. Your parents might have taught you that others are the cause for your unhappiness. They might have taught you that you were the cause for *their* unhappiness. You were the reason your mother was overworked and tired. You were the reason your father got gray hair or high blood pressure. The reason your parents couldn't take that vacation was because you had to go and break your leg and pile up all those doctor bills. You ruined things for them. These memories prepared you to blame others for your own unhappiness, as you were blamed for your parents' troubles.

Often people are confused about love because in the past they thought love meant the gratification of their own self-centered urges. Filling up loneliness with a relationship is not a basis for love. I know of two brothers who were the best of friends until they started forming new friendships and a rift developed between them. They never discussed the rift. Eventually resentment arose between the brothers out of jealousy and unexpressed hurt feelings, and they were never close again.

The examples given here are all of people who have lost touch with love. I have seen God restore love in the hearts of people, but it has never happened without the determination of the persons involved. Many times we are bent on our own self-fulfillment and plead with God to change the other person so that we can have our needs met. We need to pause and examine these feelings.

If what we do is designed to bring about our own fulfillment and safety, we have left out the main ingredient for a happy relationship. That ingredient is caring about the feelings of the other person as much as we care about our own feelings. Preoccupation with ourselves will usually distort love and keep us isolated. Our demands to be *right* will destroy the best relationship.

You are learning through this book how *not* to be an isolated person. You deserve to have loving friends as well as a loving family. You can create for yourself a loving, happy atmosphere for all of your relationships.

I constantly hear the question "What is love? I don't know if I feel it anymore." If you are to learn about love, especially companionate love, start with learning about your feelings. Ask yourself questions like the following in order to get in touch with your feelings:

1. What am I most afraid of?_____

2. What do I fear about not being in control of myself?_____

3. What do I fear about not being in control of others?

4. What do I fear about not being in control of things going on around me?_____

5. What feelings come to me at the thought of being rejected?_____

6. How do I respond when I think I am misunderstood?_____

7. When do I feel the happiest?_____

8. How do I express anger and frustration?_____

9. How do I communicate my feelings of love to those I love?_____

These questions should be answered more than once. Come back to them again and again. Feelings are never something to ignore, stifle, or be talked out of. Your emotional health and strength requires that you face your feelings. God doesn't condemn us as hastily as we condemn ourselves. His love for us includes every part of us, and that means feelings and emotions, too.

TWELVE

Learn to Restore Your Emotional Health

You are about to learn some Growing Closer strategies. This is the practical-application section of the book, where you will learn to use Growing Closer skills. Restoring emotional strength is something we often overlook—and that can be more harmful than we think.

Raye was a young working woman who called me in tears one morning. "I've got to have help *now!*" she cried. When she walked into my office later, she didn't look as desperate as her voice had sounded. In fact, she was the picture of confidence. Well-dressed, coiffed, and manicured, she moved with a competent stride, smiled brightly, and held herself with poise as she spoke.

But suddenly she burst into tears. "I'm losing it," she cried. "I can't seem to hold on.

"Marie, I lead an almost reclusive life. It's *not* exciting. I want to laugh at the people who envy me. The Businesswomen's Association voted me Woman of the Year. Isn't that a laugh?

"I'm excruciatingly lonely and depressed. I'm terrified of rejection. I have few real friends outside of my business associates. My job is stressful. I work such long hours and I find so little hope in anything anymore. I'm a Christian. I really love the Lord, but I can't ever seem to feel the joy I think I should. I'm not interested in the present and I don't have much confidence in the future."

I watched her attractive face become more forlorn as she spoke. I wondered how such a vivacious and talented woman, with so much intelligence and warmth, could have allowed herself to accept such punishing circumstances.

She told me she had gone to college and graduate school while raising her children as a single parent. "It took me six years to do what other people can do in three, but I did it." After graduating, she landed an important job with a major development firm and rose up the corporate ladder to a top executive position. But she was unhappy in spite of these achievements. "My kids have their own lives now. They're independent. They still live with me, but my role these days is just to fork over money to them. They don't help around the house, and we hardly ever see one another."

Then she said, as though anticipating my advice, "Don't tell me to take a vacation. I've tried that. It cost me two thousand dollars to listen to the kids fight for two weeks."

Raye did not need a vacation. Resting or taking time off would not be pleasurable to her. Being overworked was not her problem. The best experience for Raye now would be acceptance and nurturing by people who genuinely cared about her—a large order of companionate love.

Raye is a good example of how to become worn-out emotionally. She did not know how to restore her emotional strength. In all of her activity, she left out the importance of her own emotional health. She didn't have time for friends. *Time* was her problem, she said.

Her social life was unrewarding because she allowed no time to examine her needs and then pursue a logical and reasonable plan to fulfill them. Meeting new friends and developing enriching relationships seemed out of reach to her.

Most of Raye's time was spent working to make money

and achieve a position in her career world. The rest of her time was spent at home, where she felt somewhat abandoned by her grown children, who no longer needed her as much as she wanted them to. She resented the fact that success had not brought her the happiness she expected. Why didn't God answer her prayers?

When we are emotionally drained and our resources are depleted, with no relief in sight, it sometimes seems as though God Himself has turned His back on us. We forget words He has assured us with: "Lo, I am with you always" and "I will never leave nor forsake you" and "Many are the afflictions of the righteous; but the Lord delivers them out of them all."

I suggested to Raye that she begin some strategies to restore her emotional health. She liked that idea, but when we began talking about studying Scriptures, she balked. "It takes so much discipline and self-control to study and read the Bible every day. I don't know if I have it," she said.

When you see God as your friend and believe He really cares about you, it is not a difficult task to spend time with Him. Friendship means enjoying being together. I believe we become closer to ourselves when we become closer to God. In my counseling practice I see God, the Divine Psychologist, change lives and restore broken emotions. A relationship with Him restores and builds our sanity. We become people who can give, take, love, and understand our emotional needs in order to honor Him and glorify Him in our lives.

Too many Christians settle for less-than-victorious lives. There are too many Rayes who live alienated and lonely, and too many people who choose relationships that are not fulfilling. Many of them remain in liaisons they despise. Choosing to be alone or choosing to remain in destructive relationships is both self-defeating and pointless, especially in the light of the love of God.

Raye had been seriously hurt when her husband left her ten years before. The wound had never completely healed because she had not allowed herself to trust anyone since that time. She associated pain with love and love with pain. In order to avoid pain, she had to avoid forming intimate relationships. But she went a step further than that. She avoided people in general and never got close to anyone. Relationships represented pain to her, so her job became a surrogate friend.

If you don't like yourself, you are bound to choose relationships that will confirm your dislike. You will put up with being put down, beaten, hurt, frustrated, and alone because it proves to you what you already believe: you're not worth much. If you believe you are not worth much, you may resent and mistrust someone who thinks highly of you. You will wear yourself out with such misbeliefs. You need the Growing Closer strategies of restoring your emotional strength so you can get a clear picture of what you are doing to yourself.

Strategy #1: Set a Time Every Day to Be Closer to Yourself

Before you think about spending time with other people, it is important to spend time becoming closer to yourself. Your inordinate defenses, your fears of being hurt, your hidden drives to compete, your guilt complex, pride, and myriad worries make intimacy with others impossible. If you don't stop and take time to examine yourself, it will only get worse for you. When you aren't a friend with yourself, your relationship with God is lopsided. He wants to pour His love into you. You need to take time to receive that love and learn what to do with it. First, set a *daily* time to be alone with God. Get yourself a notebook and a pen to keep a daily journal. Look at the following qualities, which possibly have defeated you and made you feel lonely in the past:

1. fear of failure
2. enormous needs for acceptance

3. the misbelief that you aren't good enough to be loved as you'd like to be
4. fear of being hurt
5. boredom with your life and doing nothing about it
6. distrust
7. putting a need to achieve above all else

Strategy #2: Refuse to Relive the Problems of the Past

Taking time to appraise your personal values can be some of the most important moments of your life. Fulfilling your needs is necessary *today*. Your needs of today are separate from your past, and no matter how unhappy your past has been, you can think about the present now. Dr. William Glasser writes, " . . . Contrary to our most universal belief, nothing which happens in [your] past, no matter how it may have affected [you] then or now, will make any difference once [you] learn to fulfill your needs at the present time."[1]

The problem is that we don't take responsibility for our lives today. Responsibility is the main weapon in our self-worth arsenal. A definition of *responsibility* is "the ability to fulfill one's needs, and to do so in a way that does not deprive others of the ability to fulfill their needs." This ability does not come naturally. It must be *learned*.

Restore yourself now by confronting the following:

1. Separate yourself now from the past by seeing yourself on a new course. Imagine the Lord Jesus at your side on this course. He gently guides and holds you along the way. He is your friend and Lord. It is His desire that your new choices be constructive, good ones in order that you be fully blessed.
2. It is not true that nothing can change for the better, or that you've made your bed and now you'll have to lie in it.
3. If you have failed in past relationships, it is not true

that you will not be able to act differently and more constructively in new relationships.

4. It is a lie that people can't change and that "you can't teach an old dog new tricks." All behavior is learned; therefore, bad behavior can be replaced by learning healthier and more constructive behavior.
5. Do not be afraid that past pain will be repeated and that all people are alike.

Restoring your emotional strength is a skill. It is something you teach yourself. Just as learning a new language takes time and skill, so does learning to restore your emotional strength. If you ignore your need for this skill, you can fall into numerous traps, including exhaustion and bitterness. You will want to blame something or someone for your weariness.

Strategy #3: Take Responsibility for Your Actions

Shakespeare said, "Action is eloquence." It can be that and more to you if you take responsibility for your actions. Helen Keller said, "When one door of happiness closes another opens; but often we look so long at the closed door that we do not see the one which has been opened for us." You create open doors when you take responsibility; they stay closed when you blame others for closing them.

Almost always we want to pin the fault on somebody other than ourselves when we are weary of life. We think it is the fault of the hostile world around us, or the people in our immediate circle or circumstances. This puts us in a position of helplessness. It is being irresponsible.

Rather than turn to God, the Source of our psychological health, many of the Christians I have counseled blame Him for their emotionally bereft state. They feel, "If I am the cause of my unhappiness, why hasn't God sent somebody to show me the way? Why doesn't God send me the kind of friends I need? Why didn't God give me a better mate? Better parents? Better teachers? Better opportunities? If I'm unsuccessful in my relationships or my career, it's all God's fault. In summing up my failures, it's obvious that God is the one who is to blame. After all, He's the one with all the power, not me."

John was a hardworking, conscientious man who worked for the same company for fifteen years. One day, without warning, he was fired. It came as a shock to him. Then he learned that he had been replaced by a younger man who would earn one-fourth less pay. He was told that the action was part of a major cutback, and there was nothing he could do about it.

John became angry and withdrawn. He faced closed doors. He was hurt and unsure of himself. He felt that his ideals and his trust in others were shattered. His wife and children were often the target of his acrid verbal abuse, but he was hardest on himself. He decided it was God's fault for not guiding him properly. He figured God should have given him some sort of warning that he was going to lose his job. He was mad at God because he thought he should have been better rewarded for being a good Christian. How could he trust anybody again?

John could not see that he could be in control of his circumstances instead of the other way around. He allowed himself to sink into despair and bitterness. He refused to take responsibility for his actions.

John's wife was wise and loving toward John, but she refused to baby him. She wouldn't encourage his growing hostility toward life, so he accused her of abandoning him in his hour of need, of not loving him now that he was no longer working. She encouraged him to start over, to create a new situation for himself, but John would not hear of it. The Danish philosopher Sören Kierkegaard said,

> Despair is never ultimately over the external object but always over ourselves. A girl loses her sweetheart and she despairs. It is not over the lost sweetheart, but over herself-without-the-sweetheart. And so it is with all cases of love whether it be money, power, or social rank. The unbearable loss is not really in itself unbearable.

What we cannot bear is in being stripped of the external object, we stand deluded and see the intolerable abyss of ourself.[2]

You can't get closer to someone else unless you take responsibility for your actions in your present situation. You are the one who controls your own behavior. John had to learn the following eight rules in order to take responsibility for his situation. As you read them, make them practical by saying out loud, "I *choose* to take responsibility by . . ." and then fill in the sentence with your choice.

1. Stop blaming God for your problems.
2. Stop telling yourself you've done all you can to help yourself.
3. Stop imagining the world is a horrible place and you can't change it.
4. Stop making impossible demands on yourself. It only creates irresponsible behavior.
5. Stop imagining that other people should always do good to you, and if they don't they are at fault.
6. Learn which situations you cannot do anything about (such as weather, the attitudes of others, wars) and which you can change (your attitudes, behavior, and choices).
7. Tell yourself that *you* are responsible for your own actions.
8. Tell yourself that you can choose to be happy or you can choose not to be.

Emotional strength needs nourishment. Willard Gaylin writes:

We need to be aware of restoring our emotional strength just as we are aware of restoring ourselves physically by eating and resting. In order to restore ourselves, we have to be aware of our timing. If we spend most of our time in relentless labors of necessity, we will grow tired, anxious, and the unfulfilled hours pile up into a stockade blocking our capacity to love and enjoy.[3]

Gaylin says that the things vital to our happiness are activities that create a sense of pride, satisfaction, and competence. Nothing is harder on relationships than relentless work, long, dry seasons of labor, and few personal rewards. There is great truth in the statement that loving somebody means knowing how to take care of yourself, and taking care of yourself means knowing how to restore yourself.

Restoring your emotional strength means to take time to be closer to yourself and God; it means refusing to live the problems of the past; it means taking responsibility for your own actions. Raye, the woman who lived her life centered around her job, and John, the man who lost his job, had to learn how to make changes and set priorities. Their first priority was to set aside time every day to feed their hearts in prayer and reading the Scriptures. They discovered that God didn't expect them to conquer the world alone.

God restores our souls, the Psalmist says in the Twenty-third Psalm. He guides us in paths of righteousness for His sake. Restored strength is ours, and happiness is ours. But will we give ourselves permission to be happy?

THIRTEEN
Your
Happiness
Permit

A deeply distressed man named Harold sat in my office one day. He had just remarried and did not know how to inform his children, whom he loved very dearly. The children were older—in college— and both of them were considering marriage themselves.

Harold was fearful of telling them he had remarried because he was afraid they would reject him. They had been raised by their mother, although he had faithfully paid child support and spent weekends with them in the seven years since the divorce.

He had kept his relationship with his new wife a private matter, but now that he was married he could no longer hide it from them. The stress he felt was almost unbearable. The thought of losing the love of his children was more than he could stand.

I asked Harold, "Are you afraid to tell your children you're married because you're *happily* married?"

He thought for a while and then said, "Yes, I think so. All these years I've probably earned the children's attention by appearing to be an unhappy, lonely daddy. They always hoped their mother and I would get back together, but I knew that was not possible. They felt sorry for me and made me special things. They worried about me, telephoned me regularly, and never missed one of our dates.

Now that I am accepted and loved, I wonder if they'll just dump me. That would kill me."

Harold felt guilty for being happy. His relationship with his new wife was one based on mutual trust and kindness. She did not criticize him nor find fault with him. She didn't correct him or try to change him. She accepted him unequivocally. The effect this had on Harold was phenomenal. His physical problems and illnesses seemed to miraculously vanish; symptoms of hypertension and asthma left him. His job performance improved and he received two promotions in the year he and his wife dated before marrying—more than he had received in ten years on the job. His outlook on life became hopeful and enthusiastic instead of pessimistic and despairing. His one major fear was that his children would not love him now that he was no longer dependent and miserable.

Harold finally summoned the courage to talk to his children, after working through his feelings with me. He was amazed when their response was, "Oh, Dad, why didn't you tell us before? We're so happy for you." With the sons and father in the office with me, I asked them, "Do you have any fears that your father may not need you as much now?" The response was immediate.

"Yes."

"Will you tell your dad your feelings?"

"Well," the first son began, "I guess I wonder a little bit if I'll still be as important to you now that you're married. I wonder if you'll need us, or if I'll see you as often."

"I feel the same way," the second son said. "Do you think she'll like us? Will you move away? Will she take our place?"

Harold was amazed to find that his sons shared his fears. He had no reason to feel guilty for being happy.

Strategy #1: Your Happiness Permit Prohibits Judging

Often in our search for a place to belong and someone to accept us, we will strive too hard to be someone we are not. Harold didn't have to do that because his new wife didn't judge him. Judging is a serious matter where relationships are concerned. If we judge behaviors as right or wrong, evil or righteous, and our motivation and urges are prodded by this sense of judging, we will never really accept ourselves or others as they are. We will always have an eye toward "change."

Becky was this kind of woman. She tried to create the impression of a person who had it all together, but inside she felt out of touch with herself and her true feelings. She couldn't really appreciate the true feelings of anybody else, either, because she was so preoccupied with her own. When people talked to her about their feelings or something important in their lives, Becky didn't pause to listen before jumping right in with her own opinions. Becky was an isolated person, filled with opinions and fears. She didn't feel acceptance from others. She didn't experience the sensation of complete peace and contentment in any relationship. She feared she might do something wrong, or some fault would be detected in her.

How to Recognize Judging Behavior. If you say or do any of the following, you are giving a judging message which will separate instead of bring together.

- Do you have to wear *that*?
- I don't know why you're so afraid of the boss. Why don't you just be a man and march in there and ask for a raise?
- I thought you were supposed to be on a diet. Why are you having dessert?
- I like the flowers you brought—but were they out of roses?
- I think it's a waste of time to take that class, but it's your life.
- You're always on the phone. You're a real Miss Popular, aren't you?
- You're the one with the master's degree—*you* tell *me* which movie to see.

- Why don't you do something about your hair?
- Sure you did a good job, but you could have done better.
- You can't do anything right.
- When are you going to make something out of your life?
- That was a stupid thing to say.
- Why do you sleep so late? You really are a bum.
- You just can't seem to hold down any job, can you?
- The Bible says you're not supposed to take the Lord's name in vain. How terrible of you.
- You mean you're *still* working on that project? Aren't you ever going to finish?
- I can't believe you're not married yet. What's wrong with you?
- Why on earth do you want to rent when it's much better to buy?
- You shouldn't use those credit cards. You'll get in debt and then you'll be sorry.

I hope you are getting the message that this book is proclaiming. We are *growing closer.* We can grow closer, be more loving, loved, and happier if we will learn the skills of dropping the things that hurt us and adding the things that make us feel good and worthwhile. You may not think the negative things you say to your loved ones hurt, but in the long run they have a negative, destructive effect. We learn to relate in the same negative way. We accept negativity as a way of life. Put-downs and judgmental attitudes become acceptable behavior.

The people who rush into counselors' offices have judging voices screaming after them. This strategy is imperative: *Stop judging others now!*

Replace Judgmental Words With Reinforcing Words. This is important in every relationship. In child raising, reinforcement is essential. In my own parenting, I have often been tempted to say things like, "You *never* clean your room" or "Don't be dumb" or other negative statements.

I have been made acutely aware of judgment and reinforcement. I know I couldn't have raised my daughters
without this valuable and important awareness. I made
lists of ways to reinforce my children. I drew up charts and
point sheets; I gave rewards, tokens, prizes, special-events
awards; I had stickers, blue ribbons, treats, buttons, prizes
of all kinds. I was always ready to reward a good behavior
and activity. My children thrived. When I became negative or withheld praise, if I accentuated their mistakes and
infractions, the results were devastating. Communication
was assaulted, defenses went up, and arguments resulted.

To this day, these rules hold true for me. I have to pray
daily that I'll be supportive and reinforcing, because I see
the results of the punitive behavior of parents. If I'm hard
on my girls, impatient, angry, and uptight, they join in the
negative behavior and we lose something lovely. Misunderstanding must be discussed openly and without judging
words. "I feel" and "I hear you" messages must be given.

Tell your loved one these words:

- I'm not going to be judgmental anymore. Growing
  closer is more important to me.
- You're okay.
- I like the way you are.
- I like the way you get things done.
- You're special to me.

Make a list daily and add to it the things you genuinely
like about your loved one(s). Do not project ahead. ("I'll
like him better when he quits smoking.") Write only *now*
things.

Identify the Foxes. "Okay, that's all fine and good," you
might be saying. "I'll stop judging and I'll stop living in a
dreamworld, expecting somebody *else* to do the changing.
But what if I'm really in a bad situation and I'm like a
doormat under somebody's feet? What then? Do I ignore
what's happening to me?"

The answer is no. Let me tell you about Amanda.
Amanda represents many people I talk to. She came to me

looking somewhat unkempt, with circles beneath her eyes. She was twenty pounds overweight and quite self-conscious. "Why do people always leave me?" she asked. "Mike isn't the first one to leave—there were others. You know, boyfriends. They always broke up with me. But I married Mike."

Amanda's dating days with Mike gave her clues about what to expect for the future, but she didn't recognize them. "I was gaga over him," she told me. "He was popular in our crowd and I thought he was the neatest, most handsome guy I had ever met. It would be so weird: we'd go out and he'd tell me he loved me and then I wouldn't hear from him again for two weeks. It would be like that. He'd make me think I was the only girl in the world for him and then he wouldn't call for a long time. It drove me crazy."

Women marry men like this and men marry women like this. It is as though they are catching a rare bird that is too precious for the rest of the world. The woman marries the fickle, irresponsible man thinking, *I gotcha. You're mine now. Your days of wandering are over. I've got the piece of paper.*

But the piece of paper doesn't help much. The man is not about to be "caught" as the woman wants him to be. He is still the same guy he was when she first had a crush on him.

So Amanda, and others like her, threaten, smother, whine, beg: "Mike, this is the fourth time this month you've been out all night. Don't you *care*?"

Mike lost his job and started drinking more than usual. Amanda worked to pay the bills. Eventually, Mike stayed home all day, drinking and snorting cocaine. "But—he was nice to me. Sometimes he'd clean up, and once in a while he'd have dinner ready for me, with candles and everything. He needed me, he told me."

Amanda confused love with proximity. Because he was home, she figured he loved her. Once in a while Amanda wondered about her life and where she was going, but she was so consumed with worry and concern for Mike, she put those thoughts aside. She was herself only in terms of Mike and Mike's needs. She had become an extension of his neurotic, irresponsible behavior. When he walked out on her, she was devastated. He met another woman at a party and told Amanda, "She's not a slob like you are and she's never too tired for sex." He moved out and into an apartment with his new girlfriend. Amanda was left to berate herself for her shortcomings.

When we accept abuse as Amanda did, we must recognize our defeating behavior patterns. Amanda *chose* irresponsible relationships. She naively thought marriage would make Mike "settle down." She figured marriage meant owning someone. She was as unrealistic and immature as Mike was. She mistakenly thought she could be his all-in-all and that marriage would change him and mold him into her exclusive lover.

Strategy #2: Fight the Foxes

"The little foxes spoil the vine," the Bible says (*see* Song of Solomon 2:15). Foxes eat the grapes, chew the vines, and can destroy a vineyard if not controlled. Amanda was like a vineyard owner, sitting back and watching the foxes destroy her crop. Here are some points Amanda eventually learned and applied to her life. They apply to your life whenever the fox (male or female) is in sight.

- *Stop* identifying yourself in terms of what you do and who you love. Stand alone before a mirror and describe who you see in terms of *you* and your attributes, qualities, and character.
- You do not own anyone—friend, children, sibling, parent, mate—you own *nobody*. People are free entities. Let them go. Love never requires a cage.
- Companionate love is two *wholes* coming together to make a better whole. Stop thinking of yourself as

a half looking for your other half. Two halves only make a larger half.

- Don't be afraid to identify the fox. If you are harvesting chewed grapes, *you* can do the changing. Don't expect the fox to help you out.

Not everybody is in a dead-end situation as Amanda was. When two people are open to change, there is great potential for a relationship. But wisdom needs to be used when you are carrying out old defeating habits. You are a person of worth and value. No one has the right to abuse and destroy another person. You are *right* when you begin to see yourself as a person of hope and potential. The foxes won't be able to spoil the vine when you take stock and realize this.

But how can you be wrong and still grow closer?

Knowing When to Be Right and Wrong. It is difficult not to be right when you know you are. In order to have an intimate relationship, you have to be willing to be wrong. Some ways you make the other person wrong are by:

crying
lying
screaming and raving
accusing
refusing to talk
arguing
lecturing
acting rude
quoting the Bible
correcting

A woman who had been married to an alcoholic husband for twenty-five years told me, "My husband has been dry now for three and a half years. I remember all those years I fretted and lost sleep and overate while being concerned about his drinking. When I stopped fretting and began to keep my mouth shut, things actually changed. I stopped finding fault and I stopped lecturing. I stopped telling him how he was destroying all of our lives. When he was drunk he couldn't remember what I said the next day anyhow. I've learned not to lash out at him and to stop finding fault. The last three and a half years have been happy ones for us, and especially for me. I see him with new eyes. For so many years I wanted him changed. He was on everybody's prayer list as a hopeless drunk and an impossible husband and father. I began taking him off those prayer lists and putting him back on as my wonderful husband, whom I loved. He became that."

This woman's story illustrates the heart of companionate love. To stop judging and demanding to be right is a step toward freedom. We do not have the right to try to reform others to our liking. Asking for change by open communication, as we discussed in the last chapter on giving and taking, is the loving way to bring about change.

Strategy #3: No "Dumping" Allowed

I don't know what "being open" means to you, but to some people it means being able to say anything they please, including how bad or dumb or wrong the other person is. Growing closer says that is a no-no. Growing closer means *no dumping*. Growing closer is discovering, exploring, and sharing feelings, ideas, values, and experiences.

Here are some "dumping" examples:

Dick is feeling upset about something that happened today. Jane has a sympathetic ear, so Dick begins dumping. Key expressions are: "I hate that job. I feel so rotten. People are so rotten. I don't know what's wrong with me. I'm tense. I hate—I'm feeling awful—life stinks—why me?" All these words are "dumping" words. They are negative and they belong in a garbage barrel, not in a conversation with a loved one.

If you are feeling bad, look at the words you are telling yourself. You do not feel bad because of things that happened to you. You feel bad because of what you *tell* yourself about what happened to you. (Read *Telling Yourself the Truth*[1] from cover to cover.) No relationship can tolerate much dumping. Sooner or later the other partner wants relief.

Here is a Growing Closer checklist:

- Why would someone want to be your friend?
- Are you afraid of taking the risk of being vulnerable because you might get hurt?
- Do you treat your friends shabbily because of your own lack of self-appreciation and self-worth?
- Do your friends fill the void within you? (Only God fills voids.)
- Do you make time for friends even amid a busy schedule, tension, and stress?
- Are you able to express appreciation and affection without fear of intimacy?

These questions take time to answer. You might share them with someone else for added self-discovery and understanding.

Strategy #4: Know How to Avoid Avoidance

Avoidance can be a coping technique, a way of getting out of dealing creatively with conflict. It is a way of handling anger, too. If you are afraid to express anger, you can turn it inward and turn off. Your emotions are not turned off, however, and they will surface elsewhere. You can stay helpless by avoiding action. You can remain passive as a means to avoid trouble.

Avoidance, passivity, and inactivity are three deadly weapons against closeness. "The problem isn't mine," avoidance says. "Let someone else solve all the problems." A relationship takes the understanding and awareness of two people, not one.

"I'll just sit calmly and do nothing," means that at best

the passive person can only live on the strength of someone else's decisions.

It is difficult to get close to a person who avoids pain and conflict. It is as difficult as trying to get close to an angry and embittered person. When you try to get close to a passive person, you only see yourself reflected back. You will be met with flattery, not genuine respect.

Here are ways to combat avoidance behavior. Tell yourself the following:

I can handle conflict. Mistakes are never final. The Lord Jesus is with me and He has promised me I don't have to remain the old noncommunicating, fearful person I used to be. "For I am a new creature in Christ: old things have passed away and behold, all things are become new" (*see* 2 Corinthians 5:17).

> Remember ye not the former things, neither consider the things of old. Behold, I will do a new thing; now it shall spring forth; shall ye not know it? I will even make a way in the wilderness, and rivers in the desert.
>
> Isaiah 43:18, 19

One of the things that surprises me is that many people expect growing closer to be easy, something that should just "happen." Actually, growing closer is a skill. If you are to develop and keep companionate love, you need skills. The relationships you invest time and skill in become enriched and happier relationships to treasure all of your life. When you fail to nurture a friendship, or fail in the areas we talk about in this book, you lose closeness. When you withhold your best, you make the other person the poorer.

Throughout this book we have examined what I believe are the very best and most important ways of growing closer. But there is another vitally important aspect of communicating that we cannot overlook when we are building intimacy. Not only can you build or destroy relationships with your words but you can also build or destroy *without* words. In order for companionate love to thrive between two people, understanding nonverbal language is important. Everything you do in life is affected by what you say nonverbally. Perhaps, of every language in the world, body language talks the loudest.

FOURTEEN

Why Body Language Talks Loudest

Understanding Your Nonverbal Messages

Not long ago I was sitting in a crowded airport waiting for a flight connection. Near me stood a mother and her college-age daughter, saying good-bye to each other. I couldn't help but observe what was going on. The mother said, "Take care of yourself now, dear." The daughter answered, "Sure, Mother. You, too."

The mother said, "I want you to call if you need anything at all. Anything."

"Sure, Mother. Take care of yourself."

"Call collect if you have to."

"Sure, Mother. Well, I guess I should get on the plane." (The plane wasn't boarding yet.)

"Have you got everything?"

"Sure. I'll call if I need anything."

The words they spoke and the nonverbal communication they were giving were quite different. The words they spoke were cold and aloof, but their body language said something else. The mother leaned in toward her daughter, picking at the girl's sweater with her fingers. The daughter's body was compliant, leaning toward her mother. Their eyes were downcast and moist. The daughter's arms were at her sides, indicating her openness to her mother, and the mother's were open and reaching toward her daughter. But they didn't touch. Here were two people who wanted to communicate, but for their own reasons weren't. I had to force myself not to intrude into their private drama with, "For heaven's sake, hug and say *I love you.*"

Did you know that over 70 percent of our communication is nonverbal? You communicate your feelings and attitudes more by your look and stance than by your words. This is why it is important to know the skills of communicating with words *and* without words. If you're a shy person who finds conversation difficult, you may give the impression you don't like people. Your shyness may show by your poor eye contact and closed stance. Without your knowing it, you are saying, "Don't talk to me. I don't have much to say and I don't want to talk to you."

Your Face

Your face says more than you know. It writes more books in a day than the most prolific author pens in a year. Your face is always giving a message, whether you know it or not. Your Growing Closer expression says, "I am open to communicating with you." But when you frown or furrow your brow, even if you think that is your "intellectual look," the message you give is one of disapproval, suspicion, and "keep away from me."

A warm smile is a nonverbal communication that says to the other person, "I am receptive to you." The friendly messages that you wear on your face will attract friendly gestures toward you. When you are engaged in conversation, be sure your face is not twisted in a scowl because you are biting your lip or chewing the inside of your mouth.

Another point to always remember is to let your body agree with the words you are speaking. If you are about to say something that is very important to you, don't say it over your shoulder or looking away from your partner. Face him or her squarely, shoulders facing shoulders and eyes meeting eyes. Your body stance says, "What I am about to say is very important to me, so I hope you'll listen to me."

Your Eyes

Your eyes, called the windows of your soul, literally do reveal what you're thinking and what you have to say. By their eyes alone you could tell that the mother and daughter in the airport wanted to be loved by each other. The teary eyes, warm but averted, said, "Please love me." Eyes that avoid looking into the eyes of someone else, eyes that flutter or are cast down, eyes that dart about the room, eyes that roll in disparagement, eyes that twinkle with laughter and have a special glint while in your presence, are all giving messages.

When you are talking to people be sure to look them straight in the eye. But don't look too long because that's staring, and that makes people feel uncomfortable and suspicious. At the same time, averting your eyes and not looking right into the eyes of your partner is also suspicious. Avoiding eye contact says, "I'm not interested." It can also say, "I'm dishonest or bored with the person I am with." If you like a person, you can let it be known by looking at him or her while engaged in conversation and by keeping a soft expression on your face. Your eyes and your face should tell the other person, "I am open to what you have to say."

You can tell how a person feels about you by watching his eyes. You can learn his true feelings about what is going on around him by watching his eyes. The eyes reveal what people are thinking and feeling, if you know how to observe them. When a person agrees with you, his pupils expand. Studies have shown that pupils expand when men are looking at women they find attractive. Magicians have said they can tell which card in a deck a person is thinking of because his pupils will enlarge at the sight of the card.

The pupils of the eyes become small when the person you are with is indifferent to you, the situation, conversation, or environment. If the person does not agree with you or if you have offended him or her in some way, the pupils of the eyes will contract. The person may not tell you he is offended, but his eyes will.

You can tell when a person is lying by watching his eye movements. When we lie our eye movements are about twelve times faster than the usual rate. When a person blinks excessively, we get the message that he is in distress or may not be truthful.

Your Stance

People respond to the messages we give, whether verbal or nonverbal. When you cross your arms in front of you, you are in a closed stance or posture. When you sit with your arms and legs crossed, you are in a closed posture. Your hands should not be at your mouth, as though you are in deep thought or as if you are going to eat your knuckles. Keep your face and body stance open, as though you are listening, not holding your stomach intact with your arms.

Have you ever noticed the body stance of two children who are fighting? Their bodies are bent and tense, their fists may be clenched, their knees are bent, and they are rounded over, ready for anything. Their mother watches unhappily as they shout at each other, but actually the shouting isn't necessary—their bodies say it all. A tense, hostile stance is affected with the head protruding forward, the neck stiff; fists are clenched and the whole posture looks something like a cat ready to spring.

Watch two people who are arguing. Watch their faces. Watch the way they move. Their movements are sharp and quick. The muscles of the face are tight. Eyes flare and you receive a definite "I'm angry" message from their nonverbal language alone.

The Importance of a Smile

Smiling is another key to what a person is really feeling. A person who smiles a lot, for no apparent reason, is usually masking anger. Therapists will hear patients say, with a smile, "My life is a mess and I don't really know whether I'm coming or going ." It is important to be in control of our nonverbal language. If we are angry, there is no reason to smile in order to cover it. I have heard parents mete out bitter punishments to their children with smiles on their faces. This is a double message, because a smile is supposed to express pleasant feelings. A punishment is not pleasant.

We can dare to let our faces say what we feel. Don't smile if you are angry. This does not mean that we should distort our faces into masks of fury; a firm expression would be more appropriate than a smile.

Methods of Communicating

We speak about seven hundred utterings a day, either to ourselves or to others. Some people speak as many as twelve thousand sentences every day, the equivalent of two novels per day. But even though we say so much, our nonverbal language speaks more loudly than our words do. We have to be conscious of this and choose to communicate loving and approving messages to those who are close to us—with or without words.

Jesus communicated a powerful nonverbal message when He sat writing in the dirt with a stick, not saying a word, as a horrible scene of judgment went on before Him. The penalty for adultery was to stone the accused to death. A woman was dragged before Him, having been caught in the very act. The crowd was enraged, and the Pharisees figured this would be a good time to trap Jesus. How could He defy the law? But Jesus' whole body was at peace. His face held no fear; His body could not have been hunched up in tension because the Bible says He simply sat quietly writing with a stick in the dirt.

When He looked up He said calmly, "Which of you has never committed a sin?" When no one could step forward, He said, "Whoever here has not committed a sin, throw the first stone."

As the disgruntled crowd dispersed and the unhappy Pharisees moved on, Jesus asked the woman where her accusers were. She said there were none, and Jesus answered, "I do not accuse you, either. Go your way and sin no more" (see John 8:1–11).

The message Jesus gave was one of confidence and control. He was not intimidated by the Pharisees. He was so confident He didn't even look at them when they addressed Him. He played with a stick and wrote in the dirt. Jesus' message was spoken not only by His words but also by the way He looked, carried Himself, and by His actions.

Jesus gave nonverbal messages quite often. One day He was on a boat on the Sea of Galilee when a storm hit. Though it was a ferocious storm, He was asleep in the stern. The driving rain didn't bother Him a bit. It was Peter who woke Him in panic because the waves were breaking over the sides and filling the boat. Peter cried out that they were going to drown in the storm. Jesus asked where his faith was and then simply stood up, raised His arms, and reproached the wind and waves. Suddenly the storm stopped as quickly as it had begun. Jesus had given a powerful message by His calm behavior. What could be more obvious than falling asleep in the very face of death? He could have said in words, "I'm not a bit worried about this storm," but instead he said it far more dramatically, nonverbally. Then He said to His disciples, "Haven't you learned to trust yet?" (See Mark 4:35–40.)

Growing Closer Nonverbal Language Strategy

Communicate by listening. Listening to people means more than just being quiet while they are speaking, even though this is far more common than really hearing what is being said. Most of the time we are thinking about what we are going to say instead of really listening to what is being said. Talking to someone verbally or nonverbally is your way of sharing something you want another person to know. If you tell me something and my eyes are fluttering in another direction, or I am sitting on the edge of my chair as though I'm ready to leave at any second, you will get the message that I really don't care what you are saying. If I look you in the eye and nod my head as you speak, indicating I understand what you are saying, I am signaling to you that I hear you.

An open posture will encourage communication and a closed posture may be intimidating. Closed posture is sitting with your arms and legs crossed and with your hands somewhere on your face. This posture tends to indicate a defensive frame of mind. Crossed arms often give the message (even if it is not your intention) that you are judging, displeased, or impatient.

A closed posture is also sitting back with your hands behind your head or leaning back with your hands over your mouth or chin. This leaning-back position can indicate boredom, whether you feel it or not. When you are listening to someone you care about, the open position is to lean forward, giving the nonverbal message "I'm interested in what you have to say." You may suppose that holding your head in your hands or leaning back with your hands behind your head, squinting at your partner, gives the impression of thoughtfulness or deep thinking, but the impression it usually gives is that of disinterest, judgment, skepticism, or boredom.

When I speak of open posture, this includes how close you place yourself to the person you are talking to. Open posture is the position in which you are facing your partner, shoulder facing shoulder, making eye contact. It is most positive when you are within communicating distance of your partner. This distance should be five feet or less. If you are arguing or disagreeing, you will violate your partner's personal space by getting too close. In conversation with an intimate friend, you can be comfortable at one or two feet apart.

Be sensitive to the other person's body language. He or she is sending you nonverbal signals, and you will become aware of them once you realize that this silent language has much to reveal.

Create a Message Without Words

Try this experiment in communicating. It ought to be fun as well as eye opening. Place two chairs opposite each other, one for you and one for your partner. Place them approximately four feet apart, with no table between. Do not touch. Use no sign language in this exercise, and don't get out of the chair. Once seated, tell your partner, using your *face* only, an important feeling you have toward him or her. Then add your *arms, hands,* and *body,* still not touching. After you have done this, have your partner do the same. Next, express the following feelings toward your partner *without words:*

1. Talk to me; I love to listen to you.
2. I'm bored with what you have to say.
3. You are an interesting person and you fascinate me.
4. I am skeptical of you and wonder what you're up to.
5. I trust you and enjoy being with you.
6. I'm lying to you but you'll never know it because I won't tell you.
7. I'm angry but I'm hiding it.
8. I love you madly.

Remember, about 35 percent of the way you communicate to other people comes from the way you speak, the tone of your voice, and whether you grumble, mutter, or yell. Your facial expressions are part of the nonverbal language you use, as is the stance of your body. When you want to convey your interest in and love for a person, listening is not enough. You must listen with body language that gives a message you care. Avoid slouching, fiddling with your hands, scribbling on a piece of paper, or scratching when talking with another person. Don't yank at your foot, rub your arm, or play with your mustache; sit in an open-posture position.

A frown can undermine every lovely thought you might have. You may think a slight frown gives you the appearance of really thinking about what your partner is saying, but you are actually signaling disapproval. A frown is never a happy expression. It is never positive. Only a smile gives the message that you are open and receptive. Listen to your friends with all of you. Allow the love of God to permeate your entire being so that you shed all masks and allow no defenses to come between you and communicating with the important people in your life, which brings us to our final chapter. Controlling your thoughts, actions, and body language prepare you for the most honest, wholesome, and fulfilling relationships—and knowing how to take as well as give.

FIFTEEN

The
Art of
Giving and Taking

When somebody complains to me how much he or she has given in a relationship, I am reminded of an old Chinese proverb about a vase with only one side: *Only the fool buys a work of art without examining all of its beauty.* Taking is as important as giving. As a counselor I listen to many stories of how one partner took too much, another gave too little—demonstrating the critical need for learning the art of giving and taking. Of all our Growing Closer skills, the art of giving and taking is one of the most important. Your vase has more than one side.

You can make yourself quite unhappy by telling yourself how much you have given and how much you haven't received. When you make a commitment to a close relationship, you become committed to the other person's well-being. This is the kind of relationship Jesus told us pleased Him. In learning the art of giving and taking, it is important to learn how to take. God gives us more than we can imagine, including eternal life, salvation, forgiveness of sins, answers to prayer, health, prosperity, and happiness. But it doesn't matter what He gives if we don't know how to take.

How to Be a Creative Taker

If we identify love as caring and being committed to the well-being of another we can understand how God's character lives in us by His spirit. God gives us the capability of truly loving because of our relationship with Him. We can learn to give of ourselves and we can learn to take from others, too. It may seem impossible to do at times, but we were each created to love and to be loved, so we can know the joy and peaceful security in intimacy.

We talk a lot about giving, but we must also know the skill of taking if we are to be successful in any relationship. The Apostle Paul said, "I have been crucified with Christ; and it is no longer I who live, but Christ lives in me . . ." (Galatians 2:20 NAS). In other words, he gave himself completely, in every way, so that the personality of Jesus could live and thrive in him by His spirit. This is our most valuable gift. Paul said in the same verse, "The life which I now live in the flesh I live by faith in the Son of God, who loved me, and delivered Himself up for me."

You can put an end to your demands, emotional tugs-of-war, needs for approval, and fear of taking. Toward the end of his life, the Apostle Paul wrote of being loved and that he *received* the love given to him. He was a taker. His fellow Christians treated him with enormous respect and love and he told them, "You are my beloved brethren whom I long to see. You are my joy and my crown" (*see* Philippians 4:1). The Christians at Philippi took care of Paul. They sent him goods and gifts because they were concerned about him. Then Paul wrote to them and said, "I have received everything in full, and have an abundance; I am amply supplied, having received from Epaphroditus what you have sent . . ." (Philippians 4:18 NAS). Paul called these supplies "a fragrant aroma, an acceptable sacrifice, well-pleasing to God."

Fear of Giving and Taking

Glenda and Rob had been dating for eleven months when they came to me to discuss the possibility of marriage. They said they were in love and wanted to learn more communication skills if they were going to "tie the knot." They wanted to know whether they had formed a poor relationship or a good one.

They were bubbly and affectionate, each eagerly agreeing with everything the other said. When I talked with them separately, it was another story. They both expressed fear regarding the relationship. It seemed like such an ominous commitment, so *permanent*. They were terrified at the prospect of making a mistake.

Here is an example of our conversations:

ROB: (*without Glenda in the room*) I don't know—I love Glenda, but there are a lot of things I'm worried about. For one, I have a problem with her parents. They don't like me. It makes me defensive. Glenda is so close to her family. I feel as if I'm on trial when I'm with them. She doesn't see that. It makes me wonder if she cares at all about my feelings. Then there's how she hates to sit and listen to me talk about my work, like last night. I was telling her about my job and what I do and she seemed bored. That scares me. What if we get married and we can't talk? Shouldn't she show more interest in what's important to me?

GLENDA: (*without Rob in the room*) Rob is a wonderful guy. I couldn't ask for a more terrific boyfriend. I have to be honest, though. I'm worried about getting married. We have a lot of differences. He likes to dominate conversations and only talk about himself. When he goes on and on about his job or whatever, I just tune out. There's no hope to get a word in edgewise. And he doesn't like my family, which is something I can't understand because they are all such beautiful people. I'm not sure if Rob meets my expectations as someone I want to call my husband.

You can see that Glenda and Rob had unmet expectations and unexpressed needs and fears, all of which they had not dared bring into the open. They were unsure about the cost of giving and taking. Their relationship could be greatly enhanced and love could flow more freely by the following strategies:

Strategy #1: Learn the Skills of Being Open

Openness has two essential rules. The first one is, *Express your feelings only. No accusations, judgments, or condemning statements.* The second one is, *In responding, do not be defensive or make excuses. Listen and make your partner aware that you are listening by not arguing, interrupting, or trying to talk him or her out of the feelings being shared.*

Here are four examples of open statements and open responses:

OPEN STATEMENT	OPEN RESPONSE
I am feeling angry. (NOT, "It's your fault I'm angry.")	Tell me about it. I'm listening to you. (I won't give advice.)
I need to hear you tell me you love me now. (NOT, "You never say you love me anymore.")	Yes, I love you! (I won't say you already know I love you.)
I'm feeling hurt because of something you said (or did, didn't do, or didn't say). (NOT, "How *could* you say that to me?")	I'm sorry you're feeling hurt. I want you to tell me about your feelings. (I won't defend my behavior—I'll hear you.)

OPEN STATEMENT	OPEN RESPONSE
I'm feeling tired and un-talkative now. Is it okay with you if I'm quiet for a while? (NOT, "Look, I know I'm not Charm City. Take it or leave it, that's just how I am.")	I give you the right to be tired and untalkative. (I won't take it personally.)
Sometimes I feel jealous of you because you are so in-telligent.	Thanks for being so open. Sometimes I'm jealous of you, too. (I won't put myself down to ease your jeal-ousy.)
Sometimes I worry that you will stop loving me and leave me. (NOT, "Promise me you'll never, *ever* leave me.")	I hear you. Sometimes I worry that you might leave me, too. When we talk about our feelings, I feel better. (I won't psychoana-lyze your fears.)
Will you reassure me? (NOT, "If you leave me, I'll curl up and die.")	Let me reassure you that I have no intention of leaving you. (I'll verbalize my love and devotion often.)

Give your partner (friend, spouse, offspring, anyone you are close to or want to be closer to) the gift of openness.

Openness means asking for what you want. Asking for what you want is a gift to your partner because it tells him or her in easy-to-understand ways how to best contribute to your well-being. You cannot depend upon intuition or guesswork to have your wants fulfilled. You give up your emotional demands in order to give and take freely. You don't lay a heavy burden on your partner or resort to guilt to fulfill your needs. You understand that you have chosen this particular relationship because you are a loving peson, and love must be expressed and experienced.

Personal success can bring some satisfaction, as can certain sensations and feelings of achievement, security, passion, and infatuation, but the experience of companionate love is an experience of give-and-take openness. In order not to isolate yourself, learn these skills now. Go back and reread chapter 2 in order to firmly plant in your mind what kind of friend you have the potential to be.

Once you make known that you are not a dependent creature, desperate for love and friendship, you can let your partner know you are responsible for what you give and take.

It is possible to be altogether dedicated to the well-being of another by becoming emotionally strong yourself.

How to Be a Creative Giver

Let your partner know what it is that he or she can give to you for your well-being. "Dear, will you please bring me some flowers tomorrow when you pick me up for dinner?" This is the opposite of manipulating because you are asking openly for exactly what you want.

By letting your desire be known, you avoid thoughts such as, *Ralph always brings Zelda flowers. Edgar never brings me any. Maybe he doesn't care about me.* By asking for the flowers tomorrow, you give your partner enough time to comply with your wish. Don't be afraid of reminding the person. I call that "cuing." You cue the other person by saying, "I'm looking forward to the flowers you'll be bringing tonight" or "You know what my favorite flower is? Roses." Ask for what you want instead of waiting for the other person to read your mind.

Let your wants be known even if it is difficult to do. "I don't want you to call me every night. I enjoy our relationship, but I'd like a little space to do different things in the evening."

In being open and assertive regarding your wants, you will avoid deceit and lying by having your roommate or parent or whomever tell the caller you're not home. You won't feel guilty if you happen to be out when he or she calls. You won't have to make excuses for not being home to receive the call.

When you want encouragement, praise, or approval, ask for it. "Will you please tell me how proud you are of me? I need to hear you tell me I'm really wonderful. Coming from you it's so special." If you don't ask for approval, you will act out your wants, and they will then become emotional needs. You'll dump a heap of emotional hang-ups on your friend which no person could ever solve or fulfill. Choose an appropriate time, face your partner, looking him or her in the eye, and say with a smile, "Tell me something nice about me." This will also promote your responding with something nice about your partner. You will avoid behavior such as sulking and pouting and thinking you are not appreciated, if you only learn the skill of asking.

If you feel anxious or fearful about asking for what you want, it is probably because you think your partner may reject your request, get angry, or be resentful.

Repeat, Don't Retreat

Don't be afraid to repeat yourself. Tell your partner to repeat his or her request to you. A high schooler told me, "My dad reminded me about five times that he wanted to go fishing for his birthday. He didn't nag, he *told*. Thank God I heard him that fifth time. We went fishing on his birthday, just the two of us, and it was a real special time." When telling a person your wants, don't nag or pressure. Let your words be specific, then step back and allow the other person to hear you.

Letting your wants be known does not mean complaining or nagging. These are blocks to the free flow of giving and taking. Telling what you want is not selfish—it is constructive.

Strategy #2: Treat Selfishness as an Enemy

Asking for what you want is an act of giving because it helps both you and your partner openly. It leaves out guesswork and unnecessary hurt feelings. Some people who have known each other for many years tell me they know one another well enough to predict their wants before they are spoken. That is the point your Growing Closer skills will take you to. I also hear about people who have known each other for many years and still say things like, "I don't understand you" or "How was I supposed to know what you wanted?" Just being together for a long time does not guarantee companionate love or knowing one another intimately.

When making your wants known, the one deadly temptation to resist is selfishness. It is an enemy of all things beautiful. Self-awareness and selfishness are worlds apart. One draws you closer to yourself and others while the other cuts you off and strands you on an island of turmoil.

These are words that indicate selfishness:

1. My life is my own. Nobody tells me how to run it.
2. I want to spend my time doing the things I want to do.
3. These are my things. Nobody has the right to tell me what to do with my things.
4. I figure a relationship is a 50-50 deal.

The above statements are selfish, because to be fulfilled as a person is to know how to give of *yourself* freely. Selfishness will not allow unconditional giving because it will always demand something in return.

Don't expect to get what you want at all times. I've seen people make demands of each other, and when the answer isn't immediately forthcoming, there are hurt feelings and indignation. "You never give me what I want" may be one of a myriad unloving responses. Of all the enemies of companionate love, selfishness heads the list.

- If you are self-conscious or overly self-aware, you'll have your own needs and wants parading before you at all times. You'll see your partner only as someone to meet selfish needs.
- Selfishness does not permit your partner emotional space. You'll get upset every time he or she gets upset. When your partner is angry, tense, or nervous, you will feel the same.
- Selfishness creates invisible enemies. "Who were you with last night when you weren't with me?" and "What did you mean by that last statement?" are examples of invisible enemies.
- Selfishness causes you to "stuff" your feelings, not expose them. You'll be too afraid to communicate openly, freely giving and taking, because you will be afraid of what might happen to you. Maybe you'll have to pay for being honest. Maybe you won't get what you want. However, the consequences of "stuffing" your feelings are worse than the consequences of being open.
- Selfishness tells you that someone else is "doing" unhappiness or discontent to you.

You are selfish when you want your partner to do what you think he or she ought to do. You are selfish when you put down and are hostile toward those people in your partner's life whom you feel are a negative influence. You are selfish when your love is conditional and when you make your partner prove himself by measuring up to your ideals.

Do you know what your loved one wants in life? Do you respond and give according to those wants? Can you hear your partner's wants and give him or her what is wanted, not what *you* think he or she should have?

Love is never a 50-50 relationship. More realistically, it fluctuates. Sometimes it is a 90-10, or an 80-20, or a 60-40 situation. In a 50-50 relationship both people would probably be asleep. One is always *giving* more and one is always *taking* more. A healthy relationship has equal giving and taking, without selfishness.

Selfishness says, "You owe me." Selfishness says, "It's *my* turn now to be getting something. I don't care how I get it."

In the case of Glenda and Rob, Glenda expected Rob to like her family. There was a conflict there because Rob felt the family disapproved of him and therefore he reacted defensively. He did this by avoiding them and making it obvious he didn't want them in his life.

Rob felt hurt that Glenda didn't show interest in his job. He expected her to show more enthusiasm when he talked about his work.

These are only two examples of their selfish expectations. The solution is not to give up on a relationship because of unmet expectations but to be open and listen to each other. The being-open strategy means *asking for what you want* and treating selfishness like an enemy. Ask for what you want so that you don't make your request a demand or an unrealistic expectation. It is not the end of the world if the request goes unanswered. God is the only one who can answer all of our requests, and sometimes even He says no.

Strategy #3: Make a Give-and-Take Agreement With Your Partner

In learning to be open, set aside time with your partner or someone with whom you are growing closer to talk openly about giving, taking, asking, and receiving. Sit down facing each other and look one another in the eye. Decide together that you will make your feelings known to each other and also that you will listen to each other's feelings. Use words like "I feel," "I want," "I need."

Rob and Glenda made a *give-and-take agreement* together in my office. They talked of their expectations and they compared notes. The agreement they made was that they would let each other know their expectations and that they would listen. They recognized that an expectation is not a demand. A demand does not bend.

After they set aside selfishness, they could enter into their give-and-take agreement, which included the promise "I will consider your wants as important as my own. When you make them known to me I will listen."

Rob and Glenda had to work on letting go of selfishness, as well as their unrealistic expectations. Glenda said to Rob, "I'm angry with you because you won't visit my parents with me," which expressed her *selfishness*. In other words, this was a demand which said, "I am emotionally dependent upon your doing what I want." This is unrealistic as well as ungodly.

Rob's expectation was that Glenda find every aspect of his life interesting. After making their give-and-take agreement, he asked Glenda, "When I talk about my work to you, will you make an effort to be interested?"

Glenda, upholding her end of the agreement, said, "I am interested in what you do, Rob. I become bored because I am *selfishly* considering only my needs at the time. I realize that I excuse this behavior by telling myself you talk too long." Glenda agreed to listen to Rob without insisting that he talk her way and only as long as she said he should talk. Rob agreed to visit her parents and to accept them, even though he felt unaccepted by them.

In dropping their emotional demands and empty expectations, this couple was able to openly give and take in their new Growing Closer awareness of each other. They focused their energy on their give-and-take agreement when they had disappointments. They didn't ignore or excuse problems without facing and talking about them.

Instead of letting love sneak up on you or "happen" to you like an accident, decide to creatively invest time and emotions in the relationship you have right now.

The real cause for much of the unhappiness in your life stems from your emotional demands and expectations, as I've already explained. If you *demand* that someone you are close to *never* criticize you, when something critical is said you will probably become angry and hurt. What was said to you is not the cause of your anger. Your demands are at the root. You cannot demand any behavior from another person. You can *ask*.

Demands will rob you of a full and happy life with loving relationships. They will also rob you of appreciating yourself. You expect the world to make you happy and to do exactly as you demand. That is not possible and it is irresponsible. When your demands are not met you become hurt, angry, and disconnected from others. Eventually, you start giving "Stay away from me" messages and "I don't want to be hurt again" cues.

But you hurt yourself. Demands hurt because they remain unfulfilled, and you make yourself miserable. You alienate yourself from others. When you do have an emotional demand satisfied, it is only a temporary experience and you simply become more dependent on outside sources. If that isn't counterproductive enough, your enjoyment will quickly be cut off because you will build more expectations and defenses out of fear of losing whatever good feeling you just had.

A patient of mine showed me a letter she had written to her husband. "We have learned so much about growing closer, Marie," she told me. "We were barely friends before coming to you, but now I really see Mark as my companionate lover. We have you to thank for this." I read the letter and it brought a lump to my throat. She agreed to let me share it with you.

> Dear Mark,
>
> I am glad you are an independent person and allow me to be independent, too. This tells me that you do not *need* me, but you really *want* me. We love being together and what is extra special about it is that we can also *not* be together. I want to share the best times of my life with you. I want you there for the worst times, too, because somehow then they're not as bad as I thought they were.
>
> You show me my better self and your acceptance of me gives me the feeling that no matter what happens in

this world, I will be all right. I want to promise that I will not judge you or withhold my approval of you. I promise I will never keep my better gifts for myself or withhold the beautiful side of me from you.

I am glad we can laugh and play as children and yet long into the wee hours of the night we can solve the problems of the world. With you my ideas never sound stupid and even if they did, somehow it's okay.

I am thankful that you allow me to be dumb and you allow me to be brilliant. I am thankful I am not obligated to please you or meet your demands and expectations.

I am glad I do not have to earn your acceptance. You've seen me angry and unlovely. When we witness each other's darkest moments, we don't consider them permanent.

Understanding our feelings takes us through misunderstandings. I am glad we can directly communicate our wants. I am thankful I do not have to be cute, charming, witty, or accomplished at anything to impress you. I am also glad that you bring out in me the charm, wit, and abilities that otherwise might lie unexpressed.

I am thankful to God forever for showing me a little more of His personality by developing us into the man and woman we wanted to be but didn't know how.

I am thankful that all of these things I have named are new and lasting changes which we have both made, and we are no longer the hard, selfish partners of yesterday.

I am thankful that we grew together and that, exploring each other, we discovered love is more than feeling.

I am thankful, too, that you have helped me know myself better. Because you are my companionate lover, I am a better me.

This letter expresses what Growing Closer can be. All of us can and deserve to have this intimacy in our lives. Notice the verbal as well as nonverbal skills the writer of this letter uses. Abraham Lincoln said, "The better part of one's life consists of his friendships." Can you say that? Action speaks with a clear voice in all relationships.

A man named Washington A. Roebling was stricken with caisson disease (the bends) while directing the building of the Brooklyn Bridge. He was in horrible pain and was forced to supervise the building of his life's dream from his bed. He was in pain but he never gave up. "Nothing is easy," he wrote in a letter to his son, "and nothing does itself. Character and action are everything."

These are the elements of a good relationship, and Roebling could have been building a human bridge connecting two people in friendship. It is not easy, but character and action are everything.

The song *Bridge Over Troubled Water* says:

> *When evening falls so hard*
> *I will comfort you,*
> *I'll take your part*
> *Oh when darkness comes*
> *and pain is all around,*
> *Like a bridge over troubled water*
> *I will lay me down,*
> *I will lay me down. . . .*[1]

These words describe companionate love. We can be bridges over troubled water for one another because we are acting on more than just feeling. We've learned some Growing Closer skills to keep the bridge in place and indomitable. As Christians, our relationships can become as rich as Jesus told us they could be when He said, "Beloved, love one another as I have loved you." I believe it is possible.

Source Notes

Chapter 2 What Attracts People to Each Other?

1. R. Parmelee and C. Werner, "Attributions to Single and Shared Dwellers as a Function of Living Status and Preference," *Population*, 1978.
2. Lawrence Wrightsman and Kay Deaux, *Social Psychology in the Eighties* (Monterey, Calif.: Brooks/Cole Publishers, 1981).
3. D. Byrne and T. J. Wong, "Racial Prejudice, Interpersonal Attraction and Assumed Dissimilarity of Attitudes," *Journal of Abnormal and Social Psychology* 65 (1962): 246–253.

Chapter 3 Kinds of Love

1. E. Berscheid and E. Walster, *Interpersonal Attraction,* 2nd ed. (Reading, Mass.: Addison-Wesley Publishing Co., Inc., 1978).
2. E. Walster and G. W. Walster, *New look at Love* (Reading, Mass.: Addison-Wesley Publishing Co., Inc., 1978).
3. Ibid.
4. Z. Rubin, "Measurement of Romantic Love," *Journal of Personality and Social Psychology* 16 (1970): 267, 268.
5. Allan Fromme, *The Ability to Love* (New York: Farrar, Straus & Giroux, Inc., 1963).
6. First Kings 19:19–21.

Chapter 4   Best Friends

1. Robert Brain, *Friends and Lovers* (New York: Basic Books, Inc., 1976).

Chapter 7   Masks as Obstacles to Growing Closer

1. Marie Chapian and William Backus, *Why Do I Do What I Don't Want to Do?* (Minneapolis: Bethany House, 1984).

Chapter 8   Insecurity Is a State of Mind

1. Sidney M. Jourard, *The Transparent Self* (New York: Van Nos Reinhold, 1971).

Chapter 9   The Manipulator

1. E. E. Jones, *Ingratiation* (New York: Appleton-Century-Crofts, 1974).

Chapter 10   When a Good Relationship Goes Bad

1. Ari Kiev, M.D., *How to Keep Love Alive* (New York: Harper & Row Pubs., Inc., 1982).

Chapter 12   Learn to Restore Your Emotional Health

1. William Glasser, M.D., *Reality Therapy: A New Approach to Psychiatry* (New York: Harper & Row Pubs., Inc., 1965).
2. Sören Kierkegaard, "The Sickness Unto Death," quoted by Willard Gaylin in *Feelings, Our Vital Signs* (New York: Harper & Row, Pubs., Inc., 1979).
3. Willard Gaylin, *Caring* (New York: Alfred A. Knopf, Inc., 1976).

Chapter 13   Your Happiness Permit

1. Marie Chapian and William Backus, *Telling Yourself the Truth* (Minneapolis: Bethany House, 1980).

Chapter 15   The Art of Giving and Taking

1. Paul Simon, "Bridge Over Troubled Water" (New York: Charing Cross Music, 1969).

Bibliography

Berscheid, E. and E. Walster. *Interpersonal Attraction.* 2nd ed. Reading, Mass.: Addison-Wesley Publishing Co., Inc., 1978.

Brain, Robert. *Friends And Lovers.* New York: Basic Books, Inc., 1976.

Byrne, D. and T. J. Wong. "Racial Prejudice, Interpersonal Attraction and Assumed Dissimilarity of Attitudes." *Journal of Abnormal and Social Psychology* 65, 246–253.

Chapian, Marie and William Backus. *Telling Yourself the Truth.* Minneapolis: Bethany House, 1980.

Fromme, Allan. *The Ability to Love.* New York: Farrar, Straus & Giroux, Inc., 1963.

Gaylin, Willard. *Caring.* New York: Alfred A. Knopf, Inc., 1976.

Glasser, William, M.D. *Reality Therapy: A New Approach to Psychiatry.* New York: Harper & Row Pubs., Inc., 1965.

Jourard, Sidney M. *The Transparent Self.* New York: Van Nos Reinhold, 1971.

Jones, E. E. *Ingratiation.* New York: Appleton-Century-Crofts, 1974.

Kiev, Ari, M.D. *How to Keep Love Alive.* New York: Harper & Row Pubs., Inc., 1982.

Kierkegaard, Sören. "The Sickness Unto Death." Quoted by Willard Gaylin in *Feelings, Our Vital Signs*. New York: Harper & Row, Pubs., Inc., 1979.

Parmalee, R. and C. Werner. "Attributions to Single and Shared Dwellers as a Function of Living Status and Preference." *Population*, 1978.

Rubin, Z. "Measurement of Romantic Love." *Journal of Personality and Social Psychology* 16, (1970): 267–268.

Walster, E. and G. W. Walster. *New Look at Love*. Reading, Mass.: Addison-Wesley Publishing Co., Inc., 1978.

Wrightsman, Lawrence and Kay Deaux. *Social Psychology in the Eighties*. Monterey, Calif.: Brooks/Cole Publishers, 1981.